Beyond Life
Eileen's Eternal Bond

"A journey of discovery and realisation that we are immortal souls and our loved ones are always with us"

Mike Threlkeld

Copyright © 2025 Mike Threlkeld
ISBN: 978-1-923078-96-3

Published by Vivid Publishing
A division of Fontaine Publishing Group
P.O. Box 948, Fremantle
Western Australia 6959
www.vividpublishing.com.au

A catalogue record for this book is available from the National Library of Australia

All rights reserved. No part of this publication may be reproduced, stored in a retrieval system or transmitted in any form or by any means, electronic, mechanical, photocopying, recording or otherwise, without the prior written permission of the copyright holder.

I dedicate this book to my beautiful Eileen, for without her guidance and inspiration it would not exist.

I cannot thank her enough for the help and direction she has given me during its creation.

The words in some passages are not mine but those I have received directly from her.

I am honoured to be able to give her the recognition she deserves as the co-creator of this work.

Table of Contents

Introduction	1
Finding Eileen – The First Time	5
Our Life Together	18
Eileen's Return Home	29
Finding Eileen - Again	42
Connecting Through Writing	59
Signs and Cryptic Messages	103
More Wisdom From Spirit	116
A Viral Intermission	147
Crossing The Bridge	156
Is It Just Me	162
Slipping Back	166
Believing Is Seeing	170
The Camino	173
A Change In Perspective	200
A Final Message	208

Introduction

When Eileen made her transition, I really thought my life was also over, I felt the purpose of my life had been completely driven out when she left. We had been married for forty-seven years, and life without her seemed impossible to cope with; we had done everything together, and now I was alone. The joy had been stripped away, and nothing seemed worthwhile without her. But underneath all that grief and negativity was a truth burning inside me that Eileen had not left me at all, that we were still together, albeit in a new and different relationship.

A psychic told me that Eileen and I are more than just soulmates; we are divine counterparts with an unbreakable bond, and this bond continues to burn deep within our souls, with death being no barrier to it, for death is only a transition from being physical to becoming non-physical and moving from one dimension to another. Since her transition, Eileen has been guiding me to those who can help me most on my new life path, and a whole new experience has opened up for me.

I had received signs she wasn't leaving me even before her passing when she was in that transitional state of a coma, and they continued to come to me after her full transition to non-physical.

I know that my unshakeable belief that she was around me and would contact me was, and is, the reason we now have such a powerful and amazing connection.

After Eileen and I started connecting through our writings, it was suggested that we should put our story into a book to bring comfort and hope to others. Now I am no one special; in fact, spirituality was not on my radar until late in our relationship, but what I now have with Eileen is an awesome connection, and this is something that is available to everyone who desires it. It may not be in the same form as we have, but amazing connections are there for everyone to take up. The secret is to ask, for those in spirit can only truly connect with us when we ask.

I asked Eileen if I was ready to bring this message to others:

> " The desire to find loved ones in spirit is in everyone, but many will suppress this desire for fear of being ridiculed. Those who will come to you will be ready to receive the information we give them; they will feel in a safe place and will be able to open up their thoughts amongst like-minded people. All of us go through the process of grief at some time in our many lives, and we deal with it in many different ways; some are destructive, and others will be uplifting.
>
> Our message is to those who are searching to be uplifted by this seeming tragedy in their lives, but as you know there is no tragedy when someone comes home; in many cases it is a release from pain and sickness into sublime contentment. When you speak, speak from the heart, and the truth will shine.
>
> This is a very important part of your journey, and it will have a profound effect on those we touch. Remember, allow it to flow, and I will be there to guide you.

I have a deep sense of gratitude for all those who have played such important roles in my life since Eileen's return home. In this book their names have been changed to protect their privacy, and I have endeavoured to choose names with meanings that describe their impact on me.

Introduction

My counsellor was so persistent in trying to help Eileen with her anxiety and never gave up on her. She has also been instrumental in helping me through my period of grief. My sessions with her were uplifting, and I always came away feeling so much better. I have called her Irene, as it means peace, because so often she brought peace to our troubled minds.

The second medium I saw connected so easily with Eileen and was able to bring her to me in such a delightful way. She was also the one who pointed me towards information on life between lives and, most importantly, guided me to my mentor, something that would change my life and my view of life forever. Because of her ability to connect with spirit and bring messages of comfort from the source, I have called her Jasmine—a gift from God.

My mentor is truly a bright shining light; she brought light into my life when darkness was all I could see and has the wisdom of the universe within her. Her guidance and tuition in all things spiritual have given me the tools to connect so profoundly with Eileen, and she has helped me create this amazing life I am now living. She and Eileen have encouraged me and shown me there is so much more to life than life on Earth, and they are so in tune with one another that I have named her Helena, which is another form of Eileen, and they both mean "bright shining one".

Ruth and Amy came into our lives when Eileen met them at a Bowen Therapy course, and they have been so supportive to me since Eileen's transition. Ruth is very spiritual and has psychic abilities; her energy is light and comforting. Amy has very special healing abilities; she instantly lifts the vibration when she enters a room. She is colourful and uplifting. Both have been precious friends to me, and both names I have used mean friend.

I thank all these wonderful people from the bottom of my heart for what they have done for me. And finally I thank my Eileen for bringing me the gift of unconditional love, the knowledge that we are immortal souls, and also for guiding me to all these amazing souls so they could put me on this path of discovery.

This may seem a strange thing to say, but I believe my love for Eileen is stronger now than it ever was. During our physical lives together I loved Eileen dearly, and I know she loved me. We enjoyed each other's company and were happy to spend our lives together, but I think we took our love for granted, or maybe we just knew how much we loved each other and didn't have to vocalise it. I truly loved the beautiful lady that was my Eileen, and I now carry that love for her amazing soul, who guides and comforts me. I tell her I love her every day, because nothing can be taken for granted anymore, and because it makes me feel so good to have the most beautiful connection with such an awesome soulmate for eternity.

Our hope is that this book will bring comfort to those who **think** they have lost loved ones and a realisation that we all can stay in contact with them if we truly believe and trust this is possible; we just need that absolute knowing they are with us and should always be on the lookout for their signs. We need an open mind and not put limitations on what we perceive are the ways they can come through to us, for the possibilities are endless and sometimes magnificently surprising.

When I hear the reactions of others to our story, I realise just how important this is and how comforting it can be for people to know that they are not just in this life as a one-off; that there is so much more to them than this human shell that we live in. There is no doubt that the events that have occurred since Eileen's transition have made a huge difference to me, and as a fellow pilgrim on the Camino said once she had heard our story, it gave her hope. May it also bring hope into your lives.

Chapter 1

Finding Eileen – The First Time

Our Journey Begins
Born in 1947, I was brought up in England at a time when the world was adjusting to the post-war demographic of politics, with the Cold War between Russia and the West. It was a time of conflicting emotions, rejoicing that World War 2 had ended but cautious of the new status quo.

As a child, I was oblivious to the wider implications of world politics and grew up in a modest but adequate environment. I lived with my mother and older brother; my father had left when I was very young, and I often joked that he took one look at me and shot through!

My mother was very strong; she had to be, bringing up two boys with little or no help from our father. Times were tough, but we were never left wanting the necessities of life and were always provided for. I took our situation for granted, after all, I had never known anything different, but now when I look back, I am amazed at how my mother managed with such little help. Government assistance was far from what it is today.

She did not seem overly religious, but we attended the local

Anglican church each Sunday, and the primary school I went to was also Anglican. At around seven years old, I was starting to question the church's teachings. What made no sense to me was if God was this all-loving entity who loved us unconditionally, why was he going to condemn us to eternal damnation if we sinned?

I never did get an answer that was acceptable to me, and the main message I seemed to be getting from the weekly sermons was that the only way to salvation was to attend church every Sunday and put money in the plate as a donation to the church.

It was not long before I became completely disenchanted with this approach, and when I looked into other religions, I found most worked on the same principle as the Anglicans. Each religion was touted to be the only true religion, with their God being the only true God, their teachings controlling their followers by instilling fear into them that if they strayed from the so-called "word of God," they would be banished to hell and damnation for eternity once they left this mortal plane. And yet, when it really came down to it, the God they believed in was the same God as the others, and the religious scripts generally followed very similar scenarios.

As I progressed into my teens, I would only go to church as a means to attend the local church youth club, which had weekly meetings after church on a Sunday and where we would do various activities, including putting on plays, which we presented to the public. We entered drama competitions where different youth clubs would put on short one-act plays, and we even won first prize on one occasion. Although an introvert, I found acting fun as I was able to hide behind my characters, but generally on social occasions I felt self-conscious and found it hard to have a conversation; small talk was not my forte. It was as though my brain would shut down and become blank.

After my brother, who was the driving force behind our dramatic enterprises, left for teachers' training college, I stopped attending the youth meetings, which for me meant there was no reason to go to church. By this time, I had become completely disillusioned with

Finding Eileen – The First Time

formal religions, and spirituality was not even on my radar.

I left school at sixteen without any idea of what I wanted to do in life and drifted through a few jobs until a mate told me of a job going where he worked in a camera shop in London. I got the job and this opened up the world of photography to me. The shop was a high-class affair and had the gold crest over the door—"By Appointment To Her Majesty The Queen."

For the most part, I enjoyed working there and my interest in photography grew the more I learned about it, but at that time the class system was very much to the fore and with the store being just a stone's throw from Buckingham Palace, our clients included the aristocracy, tourists (mainly American), and everyday working-class people. It was interesting to see how the different classes were catered for, and because of the gold crest, snobbery was rife; for the average citizen, it was almost as though they were privileged to be allowed to enter the store!

After about eighteen months I had had enough of the inequalities that were openly portrayed in English life and my mate and I decided we were going to see the world. We wanted to get as far from the oppressive class system in England as possible, so we booked our tickets on a ship bound for New Zealand.

In February 1967, we arrived in Southampton on a cold and overcast day. As we approached the terminal, there were the Cunard liners Queen Mary and Queen Elizabeth II towering above the terminal buildings, and between them we could see the top of a yellow funnel. This was the Italian Sitmar Line ship, the SS Castel Felice, which we were going halfway around the world on. It looked like one of the big liners' lifeboats! The Sitmar Line had the contract for the migrant run to Australia, and this ship had done many trips under the contract, so there was no reason to think it wouldn't make it this time.

When we arrived at the gangplank, she seemed to have grown a bit and looked like she could do the job, and once on board, it was surprisingly large, although at only 13,000 tons and with a carrying capacity of around 1,300 passengers, it might be a bit of a tight squeeze. The Italian crew were a friendly bunch; they were always helpful and the food was good. The bakery made the most delicious bread rolls which we took full advantage of, laced with ham and cheese!

The trip was a combination of serene, glass-like oceans and roaring storms. The first night out we ran into a storm whilst rounding the Bay of Biscay; this was our first taste of rough weather, but being 19 and bulletproof, we were thoroughly enjoying our adventure, although many on board were seasick, but this was nothing to compare with what was to greet us in the Great Australian Bight. Once we entered the Mediterranean Sea, things settled down and it was plain sailing across to our first port of call at Port Said at the northern end of the Suez Canal.

We arrived there just before dusk and as we made our way around the port area with vendors approaching us at every turn, selling everything from "Rolex" watches to knives and souvenirs, it was like entering the stage of the Arabian Nights, with the half-light, the eastern-style neglected buildings and beggars on every corner. At one stage, a man approached us and pulled out a long knife, he then asked if we wanted to buy it! We decided to make a hasty retreat back to the safety of the ship.

The following day we woke to find the ship slowly travelling down the Suez Canal. It was an odd experience, for now the ship seemed very large, travelling down this man-made waterway in the middle of the desert, passing ships travelling in the other direction at relatively close quarters. We were one of the last passenger ships to use the Suez Canal before the 6-day war between Israel and Egypt, which started in June, closed it down until 1975. Once we reached Suez at the southern end of the Suez Canal, we traversed the Gulf of Suez and the Red Sea, and as we entered the Gulf of Aden, we could see many flames from the oil wells that dotted the landscape. We arrived in what was then called the Aden Protectorate which was controlled by the British at the time of what was known as the Aden Emergency or the Radfan

Uprising, an insurgency to take back the land from the British.

On arrival at Aden Port, we were told not to go out of the city limits as there had been terrorist activity in the area. Aden was a duty-free shopping mecca with incredibly cheap prices. One of our cabin mates (there were four of us in the cabin) wanted to buy a camera so we said we would go with him to make sure he got a good deal. This place was very different from Port Said, it was obviously much richer, but evidence of the troubles in the area was all around us. The first thing we saw when we got to the end of the pier was a British army jeep with four soldiers armed to the teeth. Welcome to Aden!

A shop scout approached us to find out what we were wanting to buy and then offered to take us to a shop that sold camera equipment. We agreed and followed him across town. We seemed to be going further away from the pier, but he assured us we would be safe and eventually we arrived at the shop. We had been told that English cigarettes could be used as currency, so we had brought along a box of 10 packs of 20 which were only 1 shilling and 6 pence per pack on the ship. We found a camera that our cabin mate liked, which retailed for about £40 back in England; he bought it for £15 plus the 200 cigarettes and it was brand new in perfect working order. Pleased with our purchase, we headed back to the ship through the streets thronging with sellers and tourists, while in the background sounds of gunfire and explosions could be heard, and yet we felt perfectly safe; it was a very surreal experience.

As we boarded the ship, we looked across to the area we had just come from, and a little farther afield there was a big explosion. The contrast between the relative safety of the city and the outer war zone was extreme.

During the next two weeks after leaving Aden, we crossed the Indian Ocean to Fremantle in Western Australia. The ocean was like a millpond, so calm with clear blue skies and nothing but sea, sea and more sea from horizon to horizon. At first it was an amazing experience, making us realise just how insignificant we are as individuals on this planet of ours, but as one day rolled into the next, it was starting to become monotonous, although there were always plenty of activities on the ship.

The day we crossed the equator, a ceremony was held to mark the occasion, with King Neptune and his helpers putting on a show and issuing everyone a "crossing the equator" certificate with a promise of a safe passage on our journey.

A few days later, we were told that another Sitmar ship would be passing us and as this was the first sign of life for a week, when the ship approached, just about everyone went to the port side to watch it and our ship actually listed slightly to port. The other ship, the SS Fairstar, passed us with everyone waving and it also looked like it was listing towards us. Because we were passing each other, the speed of its approach seemed much faster than it really was and it looked odd to see such a large ship speeding past.

After sailing for nearly another week, we were told that land would be sighted around 3 o'clock the following morning, so up we got and went out to see our first glimpse of land after two weeks of nothing but sea. As we walked along the deck, we could smell the aroma of freshly made Italian bread rolls wafting from the bakery, so we headed down and the bakers were only too happy to give us a few laced with butter. As we enjoyed our little feast, we were able to make out in the distance in the dim light of the early morning the unmistakable outline of land, but it was not the mainland of Australia we were seeing, it was Rottnest Island, which lies about 18 km off the Western Australian coast. As we passed the island, the port of Fremantle on the mainland came into sight. Soon we would be able to get off the ship and explore our new surroundings, if only for a few hours.

Fremantle was such a welcome sight after those two weeks of nothing but sea and such a contrast to our other stopovers. It was a beautiful sunny day and the place seemed spotless; the grass verges were manicured and even the older buildings looked fresh and clean.

We spent our time discovering some of its attractions and enjoying our first Australian ice cream before setting sail for our next destination which was Adelaide.

It was around 4 pm when we left in fine, sunny conditions, but all that was going to change overnight. The following morning we woke to a raging storm as we had entered the infamous Great Australian Bight. The ship was only small and was pitching and rolling violently through the waves. This was making the storm in the Bay of Biscay look like a ripple, it was going to take us the best part of four days to cross the Bight and word was the storm would be with us all the way.

We went to the front lounge overlooking the bow of the ship, the ship was pitching so much, the bow was crashing into the water, and then it would rise only to crash down again. In the rear lounge we could hear the propellers revving wildly as the stern of the ship rose out of the sea, followed by a heavy thud as the propellers hit the water once again. Looking out of the dining room window on the side, we could see waves towering above us, maybe 30 feet high, they would come towards us and as they reached the ship, it would be lifted by them and the waves would pass under us. The funniest part was when we were below deck because we couldn't see the movement of the ship, yet we were being jostled from side to side, and when climbing the stairs, it would be really hard work going up when the ship was climbing the waves, but when it dropped, we would almost run up the rest.

There were ropes everywhere to hold on to, and passengers were told not to go outside, but of course, some did and came back drenched, often with bad gashes where they had been thrown about by the waves and the pitching and rolling of the ship, hitting themselves on the steel superstructure. It was lucky none were swept overboard. We eventually arrived at Port Adelaide after what many of the crew said was the worst storm they had encountered, but we were unable to dock there as it is a very open harbour and the pilot vessel couldn't get close enough because of the rough seas, so we had to continue on to Melbourne. By comparison, the rest of the trip was uneventful, but we had had such an unforgettable adventure which, unbeknown to me, was just the start of an incredible journey that would change my life forever.

In 1949, just two years after I was born, a significant event took place that would in time change the direction of my life and give it purpose. In a small town just south of Glasgow in Scotland, my Eileen was born to a Scottish father and Irish mother:

> "I chose my mother well for this incarnation, for she was as kind and generous a person as you could find. She had gone through hard times, as her first husband had died during the war and for a while she was having to bring up my older brother on her own. She was fortunate to find a man who would take on a mother and child, and my father looked after and provided for both as if they were both his own. When I was born, my brother was eight years old, but never was he jealous of me; in fact, he always looked out for me and protected me. Despite our age difference, we got on really well and I always felt good when I was with him; we had a lot of fun together.
>
> I was raised in a tight-knit community where everyone knew each other's business. My mother was an excellent seamstress and made many of my clothes. She loved children and there were always kids at play around the house. Her sister was also married to a Scotsman and lived nearby; she had a son and a daughter and we would visit each other often, but things were tough with little opportunity for improvement, so my aunt and her husband decided to emigrate to Australia with the promise of a better life, and when I was five, they left for pastures new.
>
> Over the next year they settled into their new life in Australia and were enjoying the opportunities there. After an exchange of many letters, they convinced my Mum and Dad to follow suit, and

in 1957 we boarded the immigrant ship SS New Australia to join them and start a new life in Australia.

Life in Australia was very different from my Scottish upbringing; so much space and the icy cold winters of Scotland were replaced with the heat of the Australian summers. We lived about 100 kilometres south of Sydney and, after a period in the migrant hostel, moved in with my aunt's family on a small property in the bush where they were establishing a chicken farm. We had gone from living on top of each other to the wide open spaces of the Australian bush!

My father got work at the steelworks in Port Kembla, so we moved to Wollongong to be closer to his work, the chicken farm was left behind as my cousin had an allergy to chickens, so it became impracticable to continue there. After a short while we moved to a small village about 20 kilometres south of Wollongong and moved into our first Australian home.

Coming from Scotland with my crazy curly hair and Scottish accent, I felt very different from the other kids. I couldn't do much about my hair, although Mum would straighten it from time to time, but I worked hard on losing my accent so I could feel less alien. I made good friends with a girl from Holland who also had frizzy hair, and we became great mates, probably because we both felt a little out of place; that friendship carried over to our adult lives.

School was not my most favourite of places; I was picked on a bit and so tried to keep with my friend. But I loved needlework and sewing and, with the encouragement of my Mum, became quite proficient in them. This was to put me in good stead for the future as I helped Mum make my wedding dress and the bridesmaids' dresses and also made the bridal party dresses when my three girls got married.

On the whole, life was kind to us; living in a semi-rural setting, we were free to roam the surrounding countryside and play at the lake. Although Wollongong was just 20 kilometres away, in those days public transport was limited, so a trip to the city was a big day out, and on the odd occasion we would take the train to Sydney and enjoy the shops there. We were all settling into Australian life and my brother married and started a family. In 1967 he and his family decided to go to live in New Zealand and settled down in Devonport on the north shore of Auckland. My Mum visited them on a few occasions, and in late 1968 she suggested I go with her.

By April of 1967 we were living in Devonport on the North Shore of Auckland, my mate had decided he wanted to have a look at the South Island, but I was content to stay. He had met a family who were looking for someone they could sublet a room to, to help out with the rent. I met them and we came to an agreement, my mate went south and I moved in, the arrangement went well and we became good friends. While I was there, the father's mother came out from Australia to visit a couple of times. She was a lovely Irish lady and a lot of fun, she just adored her grandchildren and we also got on very well.

At the end of 1968 she returned for another visit, but this time her daughter came with her. Now, I had never been very much involved with girls, I was really quite shy and didn't know how to approach them. I did not make friends easily and generally kept myself to myself, but when I was first introduced to her daughter – Eileen – I knew there was something very special about her. We started going for walks and I showed her the sights around Devonport. In those few short weeks we became very good friends and I was completely smitten by her. This was a strange feeling; I had always been very independent, and yet I felt I really needed this person in my life. If there is any such thing as love at first sight, this was it for me, and from what her best friend has told me, it was for her too. It was like a reunion of two lost souls.

When it was time for Eileen and her Mum to return to Australia, we said our goodbyes and agreed to write to each other. Although inwardly, my emotions were shattered and scattered – fear that I may never see her again, along with puzzlement that I could feel this way about anyone – outwardly the British stiff upper lip prevailed, and I waved them off as her brother drove them to the airport. But once in my room, I totally broke down; it felt that my world had ended and I was completely devastated, yet how could this be after just a few short weeks! What kind of magic was at play?

After I regained my composure, I immediately sat down to write her a letter, telling her just how much I had enjoyed our time together and asked her if I could come and visit. The letter was posted and in what seemed like an eternity, with questions drumming through my mind – will she reply? Does she feel the same about me? What's wrong with me? After about a week, a letter arrived and to my heartfelt amazement and pleasure, she said she would love for me to visit.

I quickly made arrangements and booked a flight and within three months I had arrived in Sydney, once again reunited with my amazing new friend. We had a great time together; her family welcomed me with open arms and over the next two weeks I was shown many interesting places, new sights and scenes to be shared with the one person I truly wanted to be with. We went to some idyllic beaches, explored the bush and discovered a connection like no other.

To be in Eileen's presence was the most wonderful feeling and I didn't want it to end, but end it must and I had to return to New Zealand for work. Before I left, Eileen agreed to come over the following June, and our long-distance relationship of letter writing and visits was now in full swing.

When she came over, we had a marvellous time together, getting to know each other and doing some sightseeing and looking at engagement rings. We wrote constantly when we were not together, answering each other's letters as soon as we received them, making plans, and all the time our bond was becoming stronger.

Over the next six months I had a jeweller make a ring similar to one that she liked, and in December I visited Eileen and stayed over at Christmas. The ring was burning a hole in my pocket and I was so nervous that it took me quite a while to pluck up the courage to propose. I don't know what I was worrying about as we had been looking at rings, but I was trying to find the "right time", whenever that may be!

Eventually, in January 1970, in her parents' lounge room, I proposed to her; to my absolute delight and relief, she accepted and my dreams had come true. Six months later we were married in a picturesque church in Shellharbour on what was the happiest day of my life. At last we were truly together, bonded by our vows and we were in ecstasy. We had come together after two epic journeys that had, at different times, taken us both halfway around the world, covering a combined distance of nearly 50,000 kilometres after living just 600 kilometres apart when we were in the U.K.

What a journey, but what a prize!

> When I first met Michael, there was a familiarity about him that I could not put my finger on. I had just come out of a very traumatic experience and my mother suggested the trip to give me a change of scenery and, I suspect, in the hope that I would befriend the young man she had met on previous trips. At first I was nervous when we went for walks but he was kind and gentle, and it wasn't long before we had formed a close relationship.
>
> When it came time for my mother and me to return to Australia, I really didn't want to go. I loved being around this stranger who wasn't a stranger at all. We were both very reserved and I didn't want to display my feelings, but we agreed to write to each other when I went back. On arriving back in Australia, I had this excitement within me and couldn't wait to tell my best friend all about the trip. True to his word, Michael wrote and I received the letter in the first week back. From that moment our relationship blossomed and

flourished; the ocean between us was not an obstacle as I always had our visits to one another to look forward to.

When Michael proposed to me in Mum's lounge room, it was the culmination of events that had brought us together from birth. I immediately went to tell my Mum and Dad, who were tactfully and conveniently in the next room and plans for the big day were set into place, although Michael got off lightly as he had to go back to New Zealand for work and only had to organise the Sydney to Auckland cruise, although he did come with us to choose the lace for my wedding dress before he went.

What an amazing combination of events to have unfolded for us, I truly believe the Universe steered us along those paths so that we could be together. I had found my Eileen even though I did not consciously know I had been looking, yet from the moment we met, I felt I knew her, and there was an inner knowing that we would be spending our lives together. This was when my life really began; she gave me purpose and she gave me unconditional love, and I still cannot believe how lucky I am to have been able to share my life with her, and I am so grateful for every moment we have shared together.

Chapter 2

Our Life Together

A week after we were married, we sailed from Sydney to Auckland on a cruise ship to start our new life together in New Zealand. We moved into a flat in Devonport, Eileen found work locally and we were settling into married life. We would often go for walks along the harbour front and on the weekends, take a drive to explore the northern beaches and further afield. Our time together was just perfect and we were in such a beautiful part of the world.

For most couples there is a period of adjustment when starting to live together, but for us it seemed like a natural progression; we blended into each other's lives seamlessly and were at ease with our partnership. It was the coming together of two souls parted by time, although at the time I was totally unaware of this, for spirituality had not caught up with me yet.

For me it was a dream come true, a dream that I had not even envisioned would be part of my life. Here I was enjoying life with my beautiful Eileen—so caring, so kind, and so loving—life could not be better. Over the following year our relationship grew and blossomed and we became closer than I had ever felt with anyone before; we were blissfully happy and content with our lives. Eileen's Mum would come over and visit periodically, and we always had a great time taking her places and enjoying the sights. Eileen was very close to her Mum and it must have been difficult for her to make the move to New Zealand and leave her family behind, but she had chosen to come with me, and that confirmed that she loved me as much as I did her. Her Mum's visits were a great comfort to her.

When our first child was born, it was at a time when husbands were considered superfluous in the hospitals, so after I took Eileen in, I was sent home and told I would be rung after the birth. Our daughter was born at 3:51am, and I wasn't even rung until 7!

At that time, mothers and babies were kept in the hospital for a week and visiting hours were for just one hour in the afternoon and one in the evening, which really wasn't enough, so it was great when the time came for Eileen and our gorgeous new baby girl to come home. Eileen's Mum was on hand and helped us a lot in those first few weeks while we were learning the ropes on how to handle this bundle of joy, but when she returned to Australia, it was obvious that Eileen was missing her family, so we decided to leave New Zealand and return to Australia.

" When Michael proposed to me, I knew that when we married, we would be going to New Zealand to live and this had mixed emotions attached; I dearly wanted to be with this man I loved but would miss my family. After we were married, we had the cruise to New Zealand to look forward to; the seas were kind to us and we enjoyed the ship's facilities. When we arrived, the next week or so was occupied settling in and making our flat our home. Although I was far from my family, we were enjoying our life together, exploring the nearby surroundings and finding our special places.

I found work quickly and life was good, although I still missed my Mum especially. I never said anything to Michael, for it was his happiness that was foremost in my mind, and it was only after our baby was born and Mum had gone home that I started to struggle with this new way of life. Michael realised I was homesick and immediately made plans for us to return to Australia. Maybe I should have said something earlier, but I was really enjoying life around Auckland with the beautiful harbour and Mount Rangitoto, an extinct volcanic island that looked the same no matter which direction you looked at it from.

Our homecoming was timed to coincide with Christmas, and what a joyous time it was. My dearest Michael had brought me home without a thought of future work, but his positivity saw him find work easily. It was so good to be back and have the support and knowledge of my Mum, for all this was new to both Michael and me, and we appreciated all the help she gave me.

When we moved into our house just a little way up the street it was such a blessing; I was with the man I loved and my family was nearby. Life was so good.

We arrived just before Christmas 1971, which gave both Eileen and her Mum a great Christmas present. Eileen was so happy to be back with her family and with so much more support than I alone could give. I was so pleased for her, for all I wanted was for her to be happy.

For the next four years we were fortunate enough to be able to live with her parents whilst saving for a deposit on a house of our own. Just after we moved into our new house, we were blessed with the birth of our second child, a bouncing baby boy, so it was a busy time for us with the new addition to our family and settling into our new environment. Eileen was wonderful with the children; she was such a natural mother, and with Nana just down the road and eager to help, we were having a great time, all the while making changes to the house to make it our home. The kitchen was the first to be attacked with much-needed wall cupboards to give us extra storage space, and in 1979 it even got a bright yellow face lift on the doors and drawer fronts—very seventies! We did the work ourselves and Eileen was always there to help and do the finishing touches. She was so good at everything she did, from plastering walls to making clothes and curtains and especially bringing up our children.

Every year we would pack up and go on holiday, each time to somewhere new so we could explore this beautiful country. At that time there were no mobile phones or GPS to navigate by, so you were really on your own, and good road maps were essential. I did the majority of the driving and Eileen was a great navigator. We both took a great interest in the places we travelled to, and our children were good travellers; hardly ever did we hear, "Are we there yet?"

We travelled far and wide, towing a small camper trailer as our transitory home on wheels, staying in caravan parks along the way, which made accommodation affordable. Over the years we covered most of eastern Australia, with trips west to South Australia and Victoria and north through New South Wales to Queensland, including one trip to Alice Springs and Uluru in the Northern Territory. We saw the great diversity in nature that this country has to offer and many times were left in wonder at the beauty of our surroundings, from the seascapes to the forests, the mountain country to the plains, and the tropics to the deserts, each time a new destination and new experiences to take in.

Ten years after our son was born, we had another addition to our family; our second daughter was born. This time things had changed, and I was allowed to attend the birth. It was the most awesome experience; Eileen was so calm, and the delivery was faultless. My feelings at the time were ones of awe, rapture and excitement, and I was so proud of my beautiful Eileen. This was all the more significant as we had gone through the heartache of several miscarriages over the previous few years. For me the miscarriages invoked feelings of great sorrow, loss and sadness, but they were devastating for Eileen. The fact that we had each other for comfort and that we had such a strong bond between us was a blessing that gave us the strength to move on.

Just two years later we were again privileged to witness the miracle of a new life when our third daughter was born. Once again I was at the birth, and once again Eileen excelled; she always seemed to be in control and she produced another perfect child. How blessed we have been to have four beautiful, healthy children come into our lives.

My Eileen was the greatest mum; she relished family life and did the lion's share of bringing up our children, as I was mostly at work. This was a time when it was still possible to buy a house and live reasonably comfortably on one wage, which made it possible for Eileen to be able to stay home and look after the children, which was just what she wanted. Mind you, I don't think I would want to have swapped with her, as she did such a fine job; I know I couldn't have compared.

Our life was good, but our three-bedroom house was being stretched with our growing family, so in 1990 we decided to extend, doubling the size of the house and giving us all some space. We did most of the work ourselves, working well together, and once again Eileen's skills came to the fore. After six months of constant working on the extensions after work on weekdays and on every weekend, we had a break and took a couple of weeks off to do some touring. This was just what we needed to spur us on to finish the job, and after the best part of a year, when the final coat of paint was applied and the last curtain hung, the extensions were complete.

As the children grew up, we were involved in their activities and Eileen was always there to encourage them in whatever they were doing. She actively took part in the various school programs and was always there to lend a hand. The teenage years for each of them could be challenging at times, but we weathered the storms, and Eileen was the guiding light that brought stability back. She was mostly kind and gentle, but when she was provoked, the kids knew it was time to toe the line! All in all I think we did pretty well after hearing others' stories of teenage rebellion.

Eileen mentioned earlier that when in school she enjoyed needlework and sewing, which she said she *"became quite proficient in"*.

What an understatement! She had always made beautiful clothes for the children and herself, and when our oldest daughter got married, she not only made the wedding dress but also her own elegant outfit and a suit for me, plus she made the three-tier wedding cake and the bouquets. She was not just "*quite proficient*"; she was extremely talented in everything she put her hand to. Over the years she made wedding party outfits for several friends, and when our other two daughters got married, she made both their wedding dresses just from photos, along with the bridal party dresses and the ties for the groomsmen.

We always aimed for a healthy lifestyle, and the foods we ate were simple but nutritious. We both saw the benefits of preventing sickness through nutrition, rather than getting sick and having to take remedial action. Of course this didn't mean we didn't get sick from time to time, but we were healthy for the most part, and we followed the natural approach when it came to combating illnesses, as opposed to using drugs.

In 1979, when our eldest daughter was 8 years old, she seemed to be having some hearing problems, so we had her hearing checked, and sure enough, there was fluid in her inner ears. The doctor told us she would have to have an operation to put grommets in. This was not an option we were prepared to take, and we had read that a high vitamin A diet may fix the problem. When Eileen mentioned this to the doctor, his response was, "You may as well chant to the moon as take vitamins." As you can imagine, neither of us was impressed by this narrow-minded approach; apparently if it wasn't something he was taught in medical school, it was quackery!

So we decided to give chanting to the moon a go, and over the next few weeks our daughter was put on a high vitamin A diet, including daily doses of cod liver oil and plenty of vitamin A-rich vegetables. We noticed an improvement in her hearing after the first week and, a couple of weeks later, took her for another hearing test. The result was amazing; the test showed her hearing was completely normal. This convinced us of the power of good nutrition and we have followed that path ever since. How good is chanting to the moon!

Although I had left formal religion behind at a young age, I had always felt that the Universe and everything in it was created by a superior being of some kind, yet the gods portrayed by the various religions did not sit well with me. I couldn't imagine God, or whatever it was, to be some kind of human-type entity who would sit in judgement over us and send us off to eternal damnation if we sinned. I knew there was something, but I didn't know what.

My only slight foray into the realms of spirituality came after reading a book by a practitioner outlining some of his cases of past life regression. The information his patients gave, describing the places and events in great detail even though they had no way of knowing in this lifetime was fascinating. The case I remember best was that of a woman who was a Jew in England at the time the Christians were seeking out and killing them. She described in great detail the crypt of a cathedral where she had hidden but was found and killed. At the time of the past life regression, research was carried out, and no crypt was found at the cathedral, but some years later, when renovation work was being done, a digger uncovered the crypt, which was exactly as she had described.

This, along with other examples, was proof to me that we do indeed live more than one life. I found this fascinating and kind of comforting but still did not embrace spirituality to any great extent.

Eileen, on the other hand, had always had an interest in spirituality, and when she wanted to attend various events, I would happily go with her and support her wholeheartedly.

" In this incarnation I have seen auras around humans and animals for as long as I can remember; it just seemed natural to me and I never questioned if others couldn't see them. When I was very young, I liked to look at the pretty coloured energies that surrounded people to watch how the colours would change and reach

out in spurts just like the sun's energy. As I grew up I was not able to interpret the meanings of the different colours and was surprised to find that there were only a few people around me who could see them also. This piqued my interest and I learned the basics of what each colour meant and how it related to the person's health and well-being, both physically and mentally. I did not see them constantly, and as I got older, I had to "tune in" to see them. I had always had an interest in the spirit realm and would go to different seminars to learn more, but when Michael and I married, the processes of life took precedence, and in the early years I allowed my interest to wane somewhat; it was still there but hibernating.

When our youngest daughter asked me where her other mother was, we would go on a search to see if we could find her, all the time knowing this other mother was from another lifetime. This rekindled my interest and once school took over the greater part of their days, I again started searching for answers. I would attend sessions with a psychic from time to time, and Michael was always interested in what was said; he was at last developing an interest in things spiritual.

Our eldest daughter was very spiritually minded and we would go to the psychic fairs when they were in town; there was always much to see and do, from tarot readings to sessions on all the various aspects of spirituality. During this period, we found some of the great channels of our time, and Abraham in particular was one of our favourites.

Through his support and encouragement for my interest in this field, Michael's interest grew, although he never thought he was as spiritual as me or our daughter. He was always very supportive of all the ventures I took on, as I was for him. We revelled in helping each other discover new things and reach their goals, and in the process, cultivated an incredibly strong bond between us.

At one of the psychic fairs about thirty years ago, we were attending a group session with a psychic who would give readings to different people in the group, and of all people, he chose me—probably the least spiritual person there. It seemed strange that he would pick me when there were people far more attuned to spirituality and psychic phenomena than I was.

He told me I would take up automatic writing and become very involved in the spiritual aspects of life and death. Eileen and our daughter both thought this was great, although I thought it most unlikely I would be doing anything like that, and it was more probable that my two more spiritual partners would be the ones to follow that path. It was an interesting experience, but I really didn't give it much credence and thought no more about it.

A little later, Eileen bought a copy of "The Psychic Circle", which is described as a magical message board created by Amy Zerner and Monte Farber; it is used in the same way as a Ouija board. The board itself is brightly coloured and has the letters of the alphabet, numbers nought to nine, the astrological signs and other mystical symbols. Over the years we enjoyed many evenings using the board, asking questions and receiving information on all kinds of topics; often we would have to do a bit of research to check out the information we had received. This sparked my curiosity and I started to take much more interest in things spiritual.

Eileen kept her spirituality and psychic abilities to herself for the most part and she was very grounded; her family was of the utmost importance to her, and our partnership was one of support and encouragement. Whenever either of us embarked on new projects, the other would wholeheartedly give their support and help in any way possible. Eileen was often going to craft courses where she would find new outlets for her talents; we have some beautifully painted flower vases as a result, and of course, her sewing and dressmaking skills were outstanding. I was still keen on photography, especially landscapes, thanks to my stint in the camera shop in London, and we would often travel to the abundant picturesque locations both in our locale and when we were away on holiday and go on photo shoots.

We did nearly everything together, and when I went away for two weeks with a friend to Lake Eyre, it was the first time I had been away from Eileen for an extended period since we were married. Although I loved the trip and the scenery was spectacular, I found it hard not having Eileen with me. I would search out phone boxes on the way and ring her every night except when we were in areas where there were none. It would seem strange today to think of such isolation with the proliferation of mobile phones and extensive coverage, but that's how it was "back in the good old days", it was important to be as self-sufficient as possible, especially when travelling the outback. It was so good to be back with my best mate when we returned; I just loved being with her.

When Eileen hurt her back, we went to a number of practitioners without much success but finally ended up seeing one who did Bowen Therapy. After just one session Eileen was feeling so much better even though the process seemed so gentle, and she was so impressed that she decided to enrol in a course to learn the practice. At the course, she met Ruth and Amy who were also adding Bowen to their healing regimes. They got on well and would meet up about once a month to hone their Bowen skills and have an afternoon of practice, companionship and food. Ruth is a primary school teacher; she absolutely adores the children and has an almost pixie-like way about her. She is also a Reiki master. Amy is an energy healer and lights up the room with her cheerful personality. The three of them became good friends.

Eileen started learning the different moves, but as the classes were not held often, she needed someone to hone her skills on, so of course, I volunteered. It was a win-win situation; she was able to practice on me and I got the benefits of the therapy. To earn her certification, she needed to complete a course on anatomy and physiology, so we would work through it together and she completed her training to level four. As with everything she put her hand to, she became an expert in the therapy, and many a time she would fix my back after I had put it out after twisting the wrong way or not picking things up properly.

Our youngest daughter was the first to bring us a grandchild, and when she and her husband went into the hospital to have the baby, Eileen went with them to give them support and to guide them through the birth, and we were blessed with a cute little grandson. It was now Eileen's turn to pass on her experiences and help our children with their introduction to parenthood.

Over the next few years our two youngest girls produced two girls and three boys between them, and this gave Eileen a new focus in life as her family was her number one priority. It had been hard for her when the children grew up and left home to seek their independence to carve out their lives. Our eldest had gone to live in America, but she was only a phone call away and later we used the internet to talk with her. Eileen would talk to her at least a couple of times a week, which helped bring her closer, and the others were close by, so visits to and from were regular. She revelled in her role as "Nana" and was always ready to help with babysitting and to give advice when asked.

We went on trips together and continued to embrace this beautiful country of ours. At first it seemed odd not having at least some of the children with us, but we had ourselves, and for me, that was the most important part. Together we travelled as far north as Port Douglas and as far west as Perth, enjoying the scenery and towns along the way, absorbing all they had to offer. We visited some beautiful places with magnificent scenery; the Flinders Ranges were spectacular, and Townsville and Magnetic Island were tropical paradises. To be in such awe-inspiring surroundings and to be with Eileen was as much as I could ever ask for. Life was perfect.

Chapter 3

Eileen's Return Home

Early in 2014, Eileen contracted a stomach bug which caused her to be sick every time she ate. We did all the usual things—taking apple cider vinegar to try and settle the stomach, eating just fresh foods and reducing food intake to try and starve the bug. Because she couldn't hold down food, she decided to stop eating and just drink water, which she did for about a week and this seemed to do the trick. So she started eating again without being sick, but in that period, she had lost a lot of weight, dropping from 54 kg to 48 kg, an 11% drop in her original weight.

Having previously had negative experiences with the medical profession, we approached a natural therapies practitioner who treated Eileen and she responded well but was unable to put back on the weight she had lost. We wanted to find a healthy way for her to restore her weight, but internet searches for weight gain diets were pretty much non-existent, and the only ones that were there were not of the healthy variety. I encouraged her to snack on nuts and other light protein sources throughout the day, but she just wasn't putting the weight on and was getting extremely worried and stressed about it; this did nothing to help her absorb the nutrients from her food and was contributing to the problem rather than helping.

She became concerned that I would somehow get into trouble because she was so thin. I told her this would not be the case as we were trying everything we could think of to help her, but she was getting more and more anxious, and she convinced herself that she needed to see a doctor to get something to calm her down. I tried to persuade her to keep seeking alternatives as I knew that once she was in the clutches of the medical profession, she would be caught up in their protocols of drugs and tests. But she was convinced I would be in trouble and said if she went to the doctor, then it would be on record we were trying to solve the problem. Now Eileen has always had a severe case of "white coat syndrome"; she would get extremely anxious when she had to see a doctor and her blood pressure would always skyrocket, which was just the opposite of what she needed.

Against my better judgement, we searched out a doctor who could see her, as we hadn't been to one for many years, and we made an appointment. Eileen told the doctor she was extremely worried about her weight loss, but the doctor's manner left a lot to be desired; he was arrogant and almost belligerent in his approach, disregarding Eileen's comments and asking her why she should be worried. He took her blood pressure and as expected, it was high—around 160. We tried to tell him this was always the case when she saw doctors and it was always lower when taken at home, but he ignored us and ran some tests and prescribed blood pressure medication, with not a thought of treating her anxiety, apart from a referral to a psychologist.

The following day, Eileen was beside herself with worry. I tried to calm her down, but the medication was upsetting her and her anxiety was out of control; at one stage she was curled up in the foetal position on the couch. I felt so helpless and I hated to see her like that. The next morning she woke with numbness down her right side, so I took her straight to the hospital where she was admitted into emergency. By now her blood pressure was through the roof and she was being given high doses of drugs to bring it down. There seemed to be a conflict between the doctor's opinion of the cause and that of the hospital, but to me it was obvious that the peak in blood pressure was caused by the trauma she was experiencing since seeing the doctor.

The date was the 10th August, 2014, a date I will never forget, because that was the day when my world was turned upside down and would never be the same again.

Eileen was in the hospital for ten days, during which time many tests were run to try and find the cause of the high blood pressure, including tests on the kidneys, thyroid and various blood tests, but all came back clear. I decided we weren't going back to the original doctor and found another who seemed to be much more caring. The hospital had managed to stabilise her blood pressure after trying a variety of drug combinations, but it was still higher than it should be, and the specialist had also put her on statins to lower her cholesterol even though it was not high.

I was not pleased about this, for I had previously seen the damage statins can do, so at her first appointment with the specialist after she came out of hospital, I asked him why Eileen was on statins when her cholesterol levels did not indicate a need for them, and I could hardly believe my ears when he asked, "Who put her on them?" I told him I wanted her off them and would wean her off over a two-week period and he agreed. After more tests there was still nothing to show any cause, only opinions that seemed to have no factual basis to them.

The doctor kept changing the dosages and types of drugs to try and find a protocol that worked, and after one particular drug was introduced, that evening Eileen's blood pressure seemed to be dropping. Our children were with us and we thought this was a good sign, but during our conversations, Eileen went to speak and she could not get the words out; none of us could understand what she was trying to say. We rushed her back into hospital where they immediately stopped the drug. It was not said in so many words, but it seemed that she should never have been given that particular drug in the first place. By this time her blood pressure was passing the 200 mark and we were really concerned for her. The hospital staff worked hard and managed to once again get it down to a more acceptable level, but it was still fluctuating between 140 and 160.

She came home with a new drug regime, and the doctor felt that Eileen needed to see a thyroid specialist. After a few visits with him, he suggested Eileen go into hospital for one week so he could properly manage her medications and adjust the doses accordingly. We resisted this for a while, as her previous times in hospital had made her extremely anxious which was only contributing to her condition, but both the doctor and specialist kept putting pressure on, saying all they would be doing was to monitor and adjust the drugs, so eventually we reluctantly agreed.

They lied!

Contrary to what they had promised, while Eileen was in hospital, she was sent for a number of new tests, one of which was a nuclear medicine thyroid scan. I went with her to try and give as much support as I could. We were in the room where the scan was to take place; Eileen lay on the bed while a large scanning device was lowered to within a few centimetres of her head. No one had pre-warned her of what was to happen; I was at the other end of the room and I knew she would be concerned by the closeness of the machine. The machine operators showed no empathy at all and just told her to keep her head still.

When the scanning was over, I could see Eileen was very upset by the experience, and she seemed to have changed, her anxiety levels went to a new extreme and she was becoming paranoid about the motives of the doctors. She told me she thought they were trying to kill her during the scan.

From that day my Eileen as I knew her was no longer; she had become so frightened by the experiences that she wouldn't go out without me and most of her waking hours were taken up playing solitaire on the computer to try and stop herself from worrying. She had lost interest in almost everything, even her beloved children and grandchildren.

Over the next two years we searched out alternative therapy practitioners whilst Eileen was still taking the medications. I could not believe this was happening, we had always tried to follow a healthy lifestyle and had looked forward to long lives together, and now our world was falling apart. My Eileen was no longer the one I had known and enjoyed being with for the best part of my life; she had become just a shell of her former self. I loved her dearly as she did me and I wanted nothing less than for her to return to the happy, smart, caring, beautiful soul she used to be.

We tried all sorts of therapies to try and help her, from acupuncture to kinesiology, naturopathy to homeopathy, EFT, psychologists and counselling. I was desperate to find something that would turn it all around and bring us back to the way we were, but we were having no more success than the doctors. The only consolation was that Eileen was not enduring the constant medical tests, and that, at least, made her feel a little better. I was prepared to try anything, especially to help her overcome the extreme anxiety she was engulfed in, which I am sure was a major contributor to her high blood pressure.

We spoke to counsellors, and sadly, the first one was not a good choice, for after a few sessions when there was no improvement, she said Eileen had to try harder because she had her reputation to think of, so we gave her a miss and sought someone else. I found a listing of a lady called Irene who did brain reworking therapy, which was something we hadn't tried, so we decided we would give it a go. I called her and she said she would be happy to try and help. Irene is a beautiful soul who did all in her power to help Eileen, including hypnosis. If one process wasn't working, she would try another, and I remember her saying that she was not going to give up on Eileen. She was, in fact, the only person who was able to relax Eileen, if only for a few hours; it was so good to see her less anxious and this was more than anyone else had achieved.

I found a homeopath who started treating Eileen and his protocols seemed to be starting to regulate and lower her blood pressure. Where the drugs were not consistent in keeping the blood pressure down, the homeopathics were doing the job and her blood pressure was slowly but surely coming down. At last, I thought, I would get my Eileen back. I never gave up hope that she would recover, no matter how low she seemed to get.

During our times together, we had never really argued or been angry with one another; we would always discuss things and come to a satisfactory compromise if we had differences of opinions. But now I was getting so frustrated with Eileen because she didn't seem to want to get help; her waking life was focused around solitaire, constantly playing it, day in and day out. I knew this was the only way she could try and control her anxiety, but her lack of interest in all other things was driving me crazy! For the first time in my life, I started raising my voice to her to try to get her to follow the advice given by the homeopath and Irene, but she just seemed to have given up and was sinking further into her shell.

I had reduced my work hours to just five hours a day, from midday to five, so I could spend more time with her; she was always so relieved to see me walk through the door each night when I returned. I kept telling her that I would always be there for her and I was only a phone call away if she needed me. She was my world, and I so wanted my Eileen to come back to me. She said she wanted that too more than anything and was trying but just couldn't shake off the anxiety.

Most days when I came home, I would find her playing solitaire; conversations were becoming difficult and it seemed that it was all one way as she only replied when I prompted her. I felt I was living with someone who looked like Eileen but was a different person altogether. My heart was yearning for those happy times we once had. I loved her with all my heart. How could this be happening? Was this some kind of payback for something we had done in the past? If it was, I had no idea what we had done.

Throughout our lives we were both very private people and never publicly demonstrated our love for each other, and as time went by, we hardly ever said we loved each other for actions spoke louder than words, and we always showed our love by our support for one another. One night when in bed after a session with Irene, Eileen was a little brighter than usual and I told her how much I loved her, that I had only shouted at her in frustration and was sorry for that, and that maybe we should have said we loved each other more often. She replied, "*You don't need to say it; I know it through what you do for me.*"

Things appeared to be improving, if only by a small degree, and I thought that maybe there was light at the end of the tunnel, for not one minute had I thought that we weren't going to overcome this situation.

The days were passing; we would see the homeopath and Irene at regular intervals and small progress was being made. In the mornings we would have breakfast together and I would try to have things for us to do together, even if it was just to go to the shops and buy some groceries. We talked on Skype to our oldest daughter, who was living in America; she had been so supportive and would talk to Eileen daily for an hour or so while I did my five-hour shift at work. When I got home we would make dinner together and I would try to prise Eileen away from the solitaire and get her to watch some television with me.

On December 19th, 2016, one of our daughters came to visit with our granddaughter. She made a point of coming every Monday to spend time with her mum. Most of the time Eileen didn't show much interest in our conversations, but on this day she was talking to our granddaughter and showing her places on the maps on the computer. This seemed a good sign; maybe she was beginning to come out of her shell. I left for work after kissing her goodbye as I always did and was feeling a little more positive.

When I arrived home, Eileen was on the couch, watching the television. She smiled at me and we even had a bit of a chat. I was talking to her whilst checking emails when she made a strange sound. I looked up and she was motionless. I went to her and tried to get her to respond, but she was unconscious. In my panic I had no idea what to do; I rang my daughter and told her what was happening and she said to ring for an ambulance. I was totally freaked out and hardly knowing what I was doing, I managed to dial triple zero and get on to the ambulance service. I had started to give them information, but in my panic I must have pressed the "end" button and the call ended. I was desperately trying to wake Eileen when they rang back and told me to do a few things so they could evaluate the situation and said an ambulance was on its way. Within five minutes the ambulance arrived and Eileen was rushed to Wollongong Hospital.

My daughter arrived just before the ambulance left and we followed it to the hospital where we waited in emergency. My youngest daughter arrived shortly after and we waited for what seemed an eternity. Eventually a nurse came over and showed us into a private room where a brain surgeon explained what had happened. Eileen had had a massive stroke and was bleeding in the brain; he said they could operate to stem the bleeding, but there was a high probability of damage to the brain and there were absolutely no guarantees. We quickly agreed for the surgery to go ahead and waited—and waited—and waited.

Around three hours later, the surgeon told us the surgery had been successful in stopping the bleeding and releasing the pressure on the brain, but Eileen was in a coma and there was only a very slim chance that she would survive, but even if she did, there was no knowing what damage had been done to the brain. She was moved into intensive care.

I couldn't believe what was happening; my beautiful Eileen, the sole purpose of my life, was being wrenched from me. My world was completely shattered and I felt oh so helpless. How could this be happening? In our spiritual adventures, we had learned about the Law of Attraction and that our lives now were the culmination of thoughts past, but we had never conjured any thoughts of this kind; we had always seen ourselves growing old together. But the surgeon did say there was still a glimmer of hope that Eileen would survive and I was hanging onto that hope with every breath of my body.

My son had come down from Sydney to be with us and our eldest daughter had flown in from America, we carried out our daily vigil with Eileen in intensive care, watching and waiting for signs of recovery, no matter how small they were. The intensive care nurses and doctors were so good; they explained everything as much as they could and were trying all different regimes of drugs to try and help Eileen.

Day after day we would sit with her, hoping for a sign of improvement; we would talk to her because we knew she could hear us, telling her how much we loved her and wanted her back. She would momentarily open her eyes, and at times it almost seemed she was recognising us, but at other times it was as though she wasn't there at all. It was heartbreaking to see her that way, with all the tubes and equipment attached to her.

After three weeks in intensive care and with no sign of any changes in Eileen's condition, the doctors talked to us about turning off the life support systems. They said the other choice was for her to be put into a care home with life support in the hope that at some time she may come out of the coma, but even if she did, she would most likely not be able to function.

What a decision to have to make, to end my Eileen's life or for her to live with no quality of life. As one of the doctors said, modern medicine has a lot to answer for, as it is now possible to keep people alive almost indefinitely, whereas before technology had its way, they would surely have died and we would not be put in the situation of having to make such decisions.

As much as I dearly wanted my Eileen back, I knew she wanted me to let her go. I felt that although I loved her with all of my heart—and maybe because of that—it would be better to end the trauma and let her return to spirit.

The decision was made, and it was expected that within a few hours of the life support being turned off, she would pass away. But when it was turned off, Eileen started breathing on her own, so she was moved to palliative care. For another week my eldest daughter and I stayed with her, talking to her and telling her she had our blessing to go, for we didn't want her to endure any more pain. At 3:40pm on the 16th of January 2017, my Eileen, my love and my life, passed away peacefully.

I was totally devastated; I felt numb all over. It was as though someone had torn my heart out. What could I do? I couldn't even imagine life without her. From the moment I met her my life was given purpose, and now that purpose had been ripped away from me. I knew in my heart that she was in a better place and hoped with all my heart that she would be able to communicate with me.

The funeral needed to be organised, so our focus turned to that. My son found a very compassionate funeral director and we set up a meeting to make the arrangements. I felt I needed to speak at the funeral because I wanted everyone there to know just how wonderful a person Eileen was. It was hard to hold back the tears, but with the support of my family and friends, I managed to do it:

> "I believe I have been the luckiest person in the world. How many people can say they have actually shared their life with an angel?
>
> It is a privilege, an honour and a joy to have Eileen in my life. I really believe we were put on this earth to be together. She is my soulmate, my lover, my buddy, my friend and my strength.
>
> We travelled halfway around the world to be together.
>
> Eileen came here from Scotland as a 7 year old in 1957 and eventually lived in a little village in the middle of nowhere, called Oak Flats.
>
> I left England for New Zealand in 1967 and ended up lodging with her brother Jim and his family in Auckland.
>
> She came to visit him; we met and fell in love instantly.
>
> If there is any such thing as love at first sight, this was it

for me and from what her best friend has told me, it was for her too. It was like a reunion of two lost souls.

What an amazing combination of events to have unfolded for us so that we could get together. I truly believe the Universe steered us along those paths so that we could be together.

This was when my life really began; she gave me purpose and she gave me unconditional love.

The only other time I have felt as devastated as I do now was when she went back to Australia after those few short weeks. I knew I needed her as part of my life. I wrote to her straight away, and it seemed like an eternity before her first letter arrived, and what joy it brought me to know she felt the same way about me.

We wrote to each other every week for a year or so, and for those of you that knew her well, you would know just how hard that would have been for her.

Letter writing was definitely not one of her favourite things to do, so I know I was special to her.

We had an amazing long-distance romance for two years, with one of us travelling to Australia or New Zealand every six months so we could be together for a little while until we got married at Shellharbour in 1970.

Apart from the trauma of the past two years, my life with Eileen has been nothing short of perfection. She supported me in all my ventures just as I did for her; we did nearly everything together. As I said before, we were best buddies and absolutely the best of friends. A lot of the time, we were just happy to be in each other's company; we didn't need external influences, just the contentment that came from being together.

Our marriage was one of teamwork; we always came to agreements on what to do at any given time, we rarely argued, and we always strove to find common ground.

We were like-minded spirits, holding the same views on many of life's choices, such as health options, morality, finances and lifestyle. Eileen was also a great steadying influence on me as she would keep me in check when I got upset or annoyed about things. She always gave me good advice, which would help me make the right decision, and was always ready to encourage me.

Eileen did the lion's share of raising our children while I escaped to go to work. She loved her family above all else and when needed would dig her heels in and fight for them if necessary.

Eileen was the kindest, gentlest, most selfless, caring, and generous person I have ever met, always ready to give a helping hand whenever it was needed to anyone who needed it, and was never one to take credit for her achievements.

She is the light of my life, and my life has been made so much richer for having her with me.

Our wedding vows said we would love and honour each other in sickness and in health as long as we both shall live, and we have done that, but even after her transition, the love and devotion still go on, and until we meet again, even though she is no longer here in her physical form, as the song you are about to hear says, I should never be lonely, wherever I am, because she will always be here with me, still encouraging and nurturing and caring.

Eileen was truly an angel on earth, and now she is an angel in spirit, and I will deeply love her forever."

I would have liked to broadcast it to the world so everyone would know about my beautiful Eileen.

The physical reality had set in; I had lost my Eileen and was now on my own—but was I!

My spiritual beliefs gave me the knowing that although Eileen was no longer here with me physically, she would still be with me spiritually.

I thought I had lost my purpose in life, but now I realised I had a new one—finding Eileen. Would I find her, or was she going to find me?

Chapter 4

Finding Eileen - Again

The day before Eileen made her transition to spirit, I woke with the words of a song that I hardly knew buzzing through my head. The words really resonated with me, and I knew I had to find out what it was so I could hear all the lyrics. I searched for it and found it was a song sung by Katie Melua and written by Michael Batt called "I Will Be There". The words of the chorus convinced me that Eileen had put this song into my head.

This was the song I referred to in my talk at the funeral. I knew this was Eileen telling me she would always be around me, and it gave me hope that we could make a meaningful connection.

Just two weeks after the funeral, I decided I needed to see a medium to try and find Eileen again, or at least to be able to connect with her, so I searched, and the only one I could find was 80 km away in Huskisson. I made an appointment and went to see what he could tell me. At the meeting, Eileen was very much involved, and the medium gave me information he could not have possibly known; he told me we were kindred spirits, like two peas in a pod, and he asked how long it had been since Eileen had passed away. When I told him three weeks, he was very surprised, for he said it usually takes much longer for those in spirit to come through as strongly as Eileen had.

I came away from there feeling positive that in time we would make a strong connection, but I was so missing her physical presence. At times the grief was overwhelming; it would almost paralyse me, not knowing what to do or where to go, and I would be driven down to the depths of despair. My mind was experiencing a kaleidoscope of emotions, ranging from anger to despair to depression, and at times even a glimpse of happiness, but when I felt that way I would start feeling guilty and the happiness would quickly fade away. It was as though my mind was careering helter-skelter down a steep hill with no brakes.

If it was true what the channels say, that we decide when we are going to depart this mortal realm, what had I done that had caused Eileen to decide she wanted to leave me and return home? If we were as in love as I believed we were, why would she want to go and put me through this torment? I had no answers, only questions, and I felt so desperately alone.

I was told by someone who considered themselves to be spiritually aware that I shouldn't be grieving because I should know Eileen was around me in spirit. I couldn't believe my ears and I angrily retorted that of course I knew Eileen was around me but she wasn't here physically anymore, and there is a world of difference between having her physically by my side and not being able to touch her and see her anymore. He was so insensitive and had no idea what I was going through.

Our relationship had changed from one that was totally in the physical dimension to one that was now a combination of both physical and spiritual, and that difference is a huge hurdle to overcome; only those who have experienced this trauma can really understand the emotional upheaval it causes. Everyone is different and will react in different ways, often depending on their religious upbringing or otherwise, but we all go through what I believe are the seven stages of grief: unbelieving, loss, loneliness, depression, guilt, pain and hope, although not necessarily in that order.

At first I couldn't believe this was really happening; surely it was just a bad dream that I would wake from soon. Then the reality set in and I felt this tremendous loss. Suddenly I had lost the one person who made my life worthwhile, the one person I nurtured and cared for, and the one person who nurtured and cared for me—the one person who made my life worthwhile. Then there was that incredible loneliness, that feeling that I was totally alone even though there were caring people around me; the worst times were when I was in bed at night without my beautiful girl beside me.

Depression would set in and I had to really work hard to stop myself from being totally absorbed in my sorrow. I would get angry with the world and everyone in it, for they were all carrying on as though nothing had happened even though my life was falling apart. I was angry that there were people older than Eileen who were still alive, and then there was the guilt, that crushing guilt that would leave me in a place of complete desolation. I felt guilty I hadn't done enough to help Eileen in those last two years, I felt guilty that I had been angry with her when she didn't follow the practitioners' advice, and I felt guilty because I felt it was somehow all my fault that this had happened. The shock of the situation was unbearable at times and the pain in my heart was indescribable.

Despite all this, I never lost the belief that Eileen and I would connect; I was constantly on the lookout for any signs she was around me. After all, she had told me in that song she would always be there.

After my eldest daughter had gone back to America, I was alone in my house. My other children had their families to concentrate on and I didn't want to burden them with my grief, although I would visit often and we were always there for each other if needed, but I knew I had to do something to overcome it.

Some well-intentioned people suggested that perhaps I should sell up and move and make a new start, but we had made this place our home, we had raised our children here, and we had put our hearts and souls into building the extension. This was where I felt closest to Eileen; her essence was here, as were all the memories of the good times we had together and I wasn't going anywhere. And my neighbour was so kind; she was always offering to help and would bring meals from time to time. I was very lucky to have her nearby.

I rang Irene, who had been so good to Eileen; she said she could help me through my grief and we arranged to meet. At our sessions we would talk and she helped me with hypnotherapy and brain reworking therapy, using scenarios pertinent to my current state of thinking. Sometimes during the sessions she would tell me she could see energies, including Eileen's, around me, and from the first session, I knew this was going to really help me to at least come to terms with my grief.

There is no quick fix for grief; Irene told me if I was managing it reasonably after two years, I would be doing well. I continued to see her every four to six weeks, whenever I felt I needed her support and advice, and am forever grateful for all the help she has given me, guiding and encouraging me as I tried to come to terms with my grief and the new reality that was now my life.

I searched through my myriads of photos and found a good selection of Eileen amongst them, so I picked out my favourites, printed them in A4 size and framed them, placing them all around the house, with the most special one on my bedside table. Everywhere I looked, Eileen was with me. Every night before sleeping I talked to her with the photo in my hand. I still do to this day. I look at her beautiful smiling face and tell her how much I love her, which I figure she already knows, and how much I want our connection to be strong, and I ask her to be in my dreams and lie with me in our bed.

Not long after my daughter had gone back to America, I was having a really bad day. I was in the back garden feeling so overwhelmed with grief that I had dropped to my knees, drowning in an emotional sea, when I had my first encounter with a rainbow lorikeet. Called rainbow lorikeets because of their beautiful plumage, with a bluish-mauve head, orange chest, blue belly and green and yellow feathers, they are a small parrot native to Australia and New Guinea and, like so many parrots, are very vocal, acrobatic and entertaining to watch.

The bird flew into a tree in the next yard and chirped merrily to catch my attention, then it was hanging upside down and doing all sorts of crazy antics. This made me laugh and lifted my spirits, and I knew immediately that Eileen had sent the bird to cheer me up and to let me know she was around me.

From that time I would often have lorikeets appear when I was feeling low, and it was like an instant pick-me-up to see their beautiful colours and watch their funny antics. I would be "buzzed" when walking up the street or when in the garden; they would fly very close to me and chirp as they went by. Sometimes they would chirp so loud and close it would make me jump! There was no doubt in my mind that this was how Eileen was letting me know she was with me.

Two months after I had seen the medium, I felt I had to have another reading but was hoping to find someone closer to home. My searches found an ad for a medium who was doing a show at one of the local bowling clubs. It sounded like her shows were a lot of fun, but I didn't think I was quite ready for a public reading, yet something was telling me I should contact her and arrange a private reading. It seemed strange that I hadn't found her before as she was very easy to find this time around. I found out she was not very far away, so I made the appointment and went to see her. On my arrival Jasmine greeted me with a hug and invited me in; she was very welcoming and made me feel completely at ease, a truly beautiful soul full of the joys of life.

I was so desperate to hear from Eileen that shamefully, I was a little disappointed when at first it wasn't her but my mother who came in. Mum had a message for me, saying I needed to slow down, I was rushing everything, and I needed to let things flow in their own time. "Take time to smell the roses," she said. Mum was a very strong person, and in spirit was no different, Jasmine said she stood in front of her, taking no notice of her and delivered her message, then left.

Finding Eileen - Again

Then Eileen came in giving Jasmine an image of herself lying on a bed. After getting more details, she was showing herself as she was in the nuclear medicine scanning room and she told us how harrowing it was to be there, but now she was in a good place and all was well.

Jasmine and Eileen had made a good connection and I was getting a lot of information that validated her presence. Eileen told me she didn't want me being home crying over her and that I should engage in my new life and live it to the full; there was even a suggestion that I might search out a new partner, which was definitely not something I wanted to hear. Eileen assured me that I would not be betraying her if I did, but I had always been independent until I met her and if I couldn't have her beside me in physical then I didn't want anyone else. At one point she said I was her ventriloquist, which we both had a laugh about. Jasmine asked if I put words into her mouth; I said I may have at times, but now I think the reference to ventriloquism was more about the writing sessions we now do. I am not so much the ventriloquist, more the ventriloquist's dummy!

Jasmine told me we were divine counterparts with the closest of bonds. I told her I was really wanting to make a strong meaningful connection with Eileen and she suggested I do a course in Reiki, as it had made a huge difference to her when she was starting to connect with spirit. She also suggested I get copies of the books "Journey Of Souls" and "Destiny Of Souls" by Dr. Michael Newton, as they would give me an insight into what happens between lives.

She gave me the contact details of the lady who ran the Reiki course, and as soon as I got home I rang her to enrol and went online to order the books.

The lady who runs the Reiki courses has a beautiful energy around her; living on a small rural property, she is truly connected with the Earth and at one with nature. She is a shaman and conducts courses in many aspects of spirituality, Reiki being one of them. An amazing soul with psychic abilities and such wisdom.

The level one course was over a two-day period, the first mostly being theory and the second, practical. I loved every minute of it; I could feel the energies flowing both when I was delivering the Reiki and when Reiki was performed on me. On the second day when she was giving me Reiki in the garden, she said that out of the corner of her eye, she could see a lady sitting on a chair on the verandah watching us. She described her and I told her it had to be Eileen.

I knew this was going to help me recognise the different energies around me and improve my psychic awareness. I was hoping this would also help with my connection with Eileen who was proving to me that she was indeed always around me. When I left after the course finished, I had a feeling of elation and a tingling down my spine which lasted through to the next day.

As soon as the books arrived, I started reading the first one and found it hard to put down; the information was compelling, and some of it seemed strangely familiar to me. To find out about the continuation of our lives in spirit and the reasons we do what we do in each life was all starting to make sense to me; there was a reason why Eileen needed to return home, and in the coming months, that reason was going to become much clearer to me. After devouring the first book, I was hungry for more information, so I turned my attention to the second one which went into even more detail than the first. They were both truly inspiring books and I would have no hesitation in recommending them to anyone, especially those with a fear of dying or who have "lost" a loved one. The truth is we can't die; our core is pure energy, and energy cannot be destroyed. We are eternal beings, and the life we now live is part of the process we go through for the evolution of our soul. Knowing this, then death as we know it is purely a transition from a physical state to a spiritual state and is a natural progression for our soul.

By June 2017 I had completed Reiki level one. Ruth and Amy, who had been learning Bowen with Eileen and were both proficient energy healers, said they would help me and we could practice on one another. We became close friends and continued the afternoon get-togethers, only now mainly doing Reiki, although at times Bowen was used if necessary. They are both very spiritual, have psychic abilities, and quite often see or feel Eileen during our sessions, which was both comforting and frustrating for me because I couldn't, although I always knew she was with me.

When I was practicing and leading up to the Reiki level two course, I took every opportunity to improve my skills and would always be ready to be "the body" when my shaman teacher was conducting Reiki courses so the students could use me to practice on. It was always good to be there because the place had such positive vibes around it, all those who came to the courses were spiritual and open to the offerings of our amazing teacher. They were all healers wanting to improve their abilities for the benefit of the world around them, and their energy was captivating. For me it was so good to be around such caring people, as I did not have too high an opinion of the human race in general, but these people showed me there was light amongst the darkness.

I attended other courses on various aspects of spirituality to open up my mind to be more receptive to the subtleties of the energies that surround us all, whether from spirit or from the Earth, and to absorb this information that was new to me but was as old as time itself, all the time hoping that this would enhance my chances of finding my beautiful Eileen once again. I was on a mission with one singular goal in mind.

I knew I needed to be in touch with nature and would go for walks along Seven Mile Beach, which was mostly either deserted or thinly populated. As I walked, I would talk to Eileen, asking for signs she was with me. On one occasion I was well down the beach with no one in sight when a seagull flew over me, circled around and squawked loudly, then flew off. At another time I would find feathers on the beach after asking for signs; Eileen would always answer my call, I just had to be aware to recognise them.

My thirst for a better connection and validation that she was with me was as insatiable as that of a man who had been walking the desert for days on end without a drop to drink. I had to make this connection as strong and real as possible, for life without Eileen was unthinkable.

To further my cause, I felt I needed to go back for another reading with Jasmine, the medium. I wanted to experience that connection again and hear what Eileen had to say, so in early July I went to see the joyful soul who so easily made the connection with Eileen. It was like having a three-way conversation with Eileen giving me advice on what I should be doing. Jasmine was pleased that I had taken the Reiki course as well as having read the books; we discussed them all in detail and she said we had both been put here to ease the pain of millions around the world. Her spiritual shows took her to many different countries, and I could see that was a possibility for her as she could bring comfort to those she saw, but for me it was very unlikely. I could help those around me if they came for Reiki, but as far as millions were concerned, that was perhaps a theatrical exaggeration.

We talked about those last terrible years with Eileen when it seemed there was nothing I could do to help her even though I tried everything I could think of, and Eileen said this was all part of what we had signed up for when in spirit before reincarnating. My immediate thought was, "Are we all crazy when in spirit? Why would we want to put ourselves through such pain?" But then I thought about what the books had taught me and realised it is all part of the growth of our souls.

I was still fervently wanting my connection to be as strong as possible; I kept saying to Eileen that I wanted to see her, feel her, touch her and hear her. Jasmine then suggested something that would turn out to be life-changing for me; she said there was a course on aura reading coming up, and doing this would help me to tune into the energies and further enhance my psychic awareness.

Eileen had always been able to see auras and had tried to teach me, but without success; she reckoned I was trying too hard, always trying to force the issue just like I was now with my connection to her.

She used to say to just relax and let it happen.

I was willing to try anything if it was going to help me find my Eileen again, so I rang the number and booked myself into the course.

I arrived at the venue early and introduced myself to Helena, who was running the course. All I told her was that my wife had died recently and I was trying my best to make a connection with her, nothing more. She was softly spoken and had an empathetic nature. She said not to give her my wife's name, for she would tell me at the right time, and gave me words of encouragement, saying the course would help train me to feel and see the energetic fields we humans emit and, in doing so, increase my ability to sense the energies from spirit. She assured me that our loved ones were always around us, that we just had to reach out to feel them. I sensed there was something very special about this person.

It was a very interesting day; there were around a dozen of us, just one other man, which I found was normal when attending spiritual courses. Maybe this type of thing wasn't macho enough for most men, but I had no problem being in the minority, for I have always found I relate to women better than men, and I do find that in general, women are more attuned to their spirituality than men.

Our spiritual adviser told us how we are all from the one source; no matter where we are born or what colour we are, we are all part of the one spiritual family. The energies around us—our auras—can tell a great deal about us if we are able to see and analyse them. We did several meditations and I listened to her words of profound wisdom, completely in awe of her immense knowledge. She had been psychic for as long as she could remember and had a wealth of experience to draw from.

She set us all an exercise to show that even if we couldn't actually see auras, our inner self could. We were all given a sheet with outlines of a person, back and front, on it and a set of coloured pencils, then we were partnered with another. The first one would look at the other and, without looking at the pencils, pick one up and colour in the drawing wherever the mind guided. Then the other person would do the same. The result was pictures with scribbles on them, which looked like a two-year-old had been let loose!

But when our spiritual adviser came round to analyse them, there was a much deeper meaning to our efforts. I had coloured green down the right arm, which meant there was either healing taking place in that area or was needed. My partner said she had a problem with tennis elbow in that arm and was presently treating it. In my case, there was blue predominantly down my chest and upper back and purple down my legs. The blue indicated that I was starting my spiritual quest and the purple showed my spiritual awareness was increasing. We had told each other nothing about ourselves before doing this exercise and neither of us had actually seen the colours of our auras, but we had instinctively placed the colours where they needed to be.

Near the end of the course, after further meditations and teachings from this incredibly knowledgeable teacher, she had the lighting lowered and stood in front of a plain background, then directed us to look around the periphery of her form to see if we could see an aura. We all did to some degree; those more advanced students were able to see a lot. I could only see a glimmer of yellow around her right side near the head and shoulders, but that was more than I had ever seen before. Before I left, I spoke to our teacher and said how much I had enjoyed the course and that I would like to follow up and see her. We exchanged phone numbers and I said I would be in touch.

I left the course with a new hope that this would bring me closer to making a real connection with my beautiful Eileen. The course manual had exercises to help me to see auras, and I did them on a regular basis, but I never did get to the point where I could see the full aura, just odd splashes of colour at times. This was still better than I had done previously and I was pleased with my progress. Every step, a step towards my unshakeable goal to reconnect with my soulmate.

During this period I was regularly getting signs that Eileen was around me; I often found feathers and the lorikeets were still buzzing me. At times when I was sitting quietly at home, I would get the sensation of someone lightly stroking my hair, and a couple of times when I was at work at the hardware store, I would get a hint of perfume when no one else was around—not the sort of smell you would normally associate with a hardware store.

I talked to Eileen constantly; a lot of the time just chatting as though she was physically with me. It's probably a good thing we all have mobile phones and earphones these days, for I could be walking down the street talking to Eileen and no one would take any notice. Before mobile phones, anyone hearing me would have thought me crazy!

All that I was doing—the Reiki, the other courses, seeing Jasmine, and working five hours a day—was helping distract me from the fact that Eileen was no longer physically with me. I would put my focus on these activities and try to lose myself in them, but each night when I returned home there was the stark reality that I was on my own—Eileen was not there. I knew Eileen was around me, but I could not see her, I could not feel her and I could not touch her and that was so hard to come to terms with. I continued to see Irene whenever I felt the need, and she always managed to help me through my emotional lows, giving me positive suggestions through hypnotherapy and lifting my spirit. I always felt so much better after seeing her and she has given me such incredible support.

One evening, a couple of weeks after the aura course, I was having dinner at my youngest daughter's place when I got a text message on my mobile; it was from Helena, the lady who ran the aura course, and it said:

"You came to my aura course. I hope you enjoyed it, just a quick question, I have had a beautiful soft gentle lady by my side today called Eileen, she is very gentle. She keeps asking me to say hello to Mike. I didn't know today who she meant but tonight just now I saw an image of you. Could I be rude enough to ask does she belong with you? If not I sincerely apologize (a gentle woman but persistent)."

I could hardly believe my eyes. I immediately replied, confirming that yes, it certainly was my Eileen. I was so pleased that Eileen had contacted her, and I had just been saying that I should go and see her.

"Oh thank God. I wasn't sure and I was a bit hesitant in case she didn't belong to you, she was with me all day. She is a beautiful gentle soul, soft and very easy to communicate with. She must have been very spiritual. She is constantly with you in her light body. Keep warm and don't work so hard she says. She lays with you each night. She doesn't like much joining you at the hardware store but she enjoys the time with the family and feels joy you are continuing on your journey. She gently holds your hand. She hears you talking and references violet and roses, take care Mike."

The information was amazing, for, as I previously said, all she knew about me was my first name and that my wife had passed away recently. She could not have known I worked in a hardware store, that every night I asked Eileen to lie with me in bed, or that Eileen's favourite colour was violet and she loved roses. This was the validation I had been waiting for. Although I knew in my heart that Eileen was with me, and I had heard from the mediums that she was around, it was so good to have it verified from someone else.

It wasn't long before I was sitting in front of this intriguing lady, answering a series of questions on which colours I associated with different aspects of my life and health. From my answers she was able to get a picture of my present frame of mind. She then took me through a hypnosis/meditation, which seemed to last for only a few minutes but actually took 45! This was different from the sessions with Irene, where her sessions were aimed more at overcoming my grief; this was more about understanding the spiritual connotations of what I was going through, but they complemented each other and were giving me a broader view of my emotional status and level of spirituality.

I knew that if I wanted to have the best connection with Eileen, these were the paths I needed to follow. I made another appointment with Helena, who I can only describe as my spiritual adviser/mentor, and from that time, I saw her on a regular basis. During one session she suggested I read a book about a man whose wife had passed away and was on the search to find her; she felt this would help me as this was the path I was also following. The book was "The Bridge Across Forever" by Richard Bach. I bought a copy and read it cover to cover in just a few days; it was the story of his life and how he searched for love, found his soulmate, yet struggled with the conflict of his need for independence and his need for her. It wasn't the story Helena had described, so she suggested checking out other books by him, for she was certain it was one he had written. I read a couple more, but although they were very spiritual and inspiring, none were the story of the man who was searching for his wife who had passed.

The sessions were always very different, and I quickly learned not to have any preconceived ideas of what would happen. Helena would take me through different meditations to try and help make my connection with Eileen stronger. Eileen was becoming more and more involved in our sessions and would change the course of the sessions when she wanted to; her presence was strongly felt by Helena, and she was giving her instructions on my tuition.

One particular meditation involved me walking down a forest path, arriving at a clearing where there was a stream with a stone bridge across it. I would cross the bridge, watching the water rippling over the stones in the stream bed, then enter the forest along a path until another clearing appeared. In the clearing was a wooden hut; the door was open and I would enter. There was a mantelpiece over a fireplace, a window looking out onto the clearing, and a couple of chairs. As I waited in the hut, those from spirit would sometimes come and give me messages; my mother did on a few occasions, as did Eileen and her mother, but I was not always successful. Sometimes I couldn't cross the bridge, other times I would get to the second clearing but not go into the hut. Then there were the times when I entered the hut and Eileen came and talked to me. They were the awesome times! She always reinforced the fact that she was with me and would be until we were together again in spirit.

With these sessions and those with Irene, who also brought Eileen into her hypnosis scenarios, I was beginning to feel a real connection, for although I still could not really feel her, I knew that she was there with me, and the hypnosis took me to her in my mind.

In August 2018, after going through a hypnosis session, I opened my eyes, and in front of Helena was a set of three oracle cards face down on the floor. While I was in hypnosis, Eileen had come through to her and got her to pick the cards. She read out the meaning of each card, and they were all very pertinent to my situation, but Eileen was also telling Helena that I should start using the cards this way to better our connection. Helena said I should have a question for Eileen in mind and lay out the cards face down, pick however many cards come to mind and read their meanings, then sit with pen and paper, clear my mind as best I can, and see what answers I may receive, then write the messages down.

Could this be the way I can connect with Eileen? Will she answer my questions if I ask them? Have I truly found my Eileen again?

> From the moment of my transition from physical, I wanted to let Michael know that I was okay, that I had left the stress and anxiety of the physical behind, that I had dispensed of my broken body, and now my soul could soar. This was a tremendous feeling of a weight being lifted; I now felt free, and I was now beginning to feel whole again. It was important that I let Michael know I was with him and just wanted to envelop him in my energy,

but in the moments after my transition, he was too upset to feel my presence. I knew this would probably be the case, which is why I gave him the words of the song as reassurance I was with him and always would be, for we are inseparable; the dimensions cannot keep us apart.

As the days passed I could feel he was constantly reaching out to me, so I used the birds to try and lift his spirits and to let him know I was there. Whenever he asked me for signs, I would give them, but often he would not see them even though he was always searching. It was difficult for me to leave him, yet I knew I needed to fully return home and restore myself, which is why I guided him to Jasmine, for she would help me do this and, in the process, give Michael the validation that I was with him.

My passing was the catalyst for what needed to happen next in Michael's incarnation, for we had agreed to this process whilst in spirit between physical lives. Had I not transitioned from the physical, this book would not have been written, and it is important that the word gets out that we are indeed all immortal beings; it is only the physical part of us that has mortality.

For Michael to be able to make a strong connection with me, he needed to experience different spiritual aspects, and to this end I guided him, through the suggestions of Jasmine, to firstly feel the universal energy that was brought through him when practicing Reiki; he was also able to experience the spiritual energy that surrounded his Reiki teacher and during her ho-oponopono sessions.

He was slowly beginning to harmonise with these different energies, each step leading to the next, and it was only when his energy vibration was at the right level that I guided him, again through Jasmine's suggestion, to his spiritual mentor, Helena. The books he spoke "of—"Journey" and "Destiny of "Souls"—were all a necessary part of bringing his vibrations and understanding of the real truth to a level where Helena's sessions would have meaning for him. He once asked me why I didn't just bring him directly to

Helena. It is all about being ready—mentally and spiritually.

It was so good to see him taking on each suggestion with such determination, for he was just as eager to cement our connection as I was, and now we have this beautiful bond, which we really never lost, for it has always been with us for millennia, but he needs to be less impatient and allow the Universe to flow—all in good time; each step should be savoured as the next is looked forward to.

Ah bliss! That we are one.

When I got home I found an empty exercise book and, along with a pen, put the deck of cards that Helena had lent me on the table, ready for what I hoped would be my first two-way conversation with the one I had thought I had lost forever. Just the thought that I could make a real connection with my Eileen gave me tingles down my back; it was as though I was going on my first date with her all over again.

That night I asked my first question, would I get a reply?

Chapter 5

Connecting Through Writing

Conversations With My Angel

As I sat at the table with everything ready for me to take the first step, I pondered how I could do this thing. After all, I was never very spiritual before Eileen crossed the dimensions, and I certainly didn't see myself as some kind of spiritual guru. This was just me—no one special and with no special psychic or spiritual talents to call upon.

Was this the automatic writing that the psychic had predicted all those years ago? And what was automatic writing anyway? Do I sit and wait for the pen to move once I have asked my question? How does it work, and will it really happen? I almost got up and left because I thought there was no way I was going to be able to do this, and if that happened, it would be as though what little connection I had with Eileen might be lost, and I would never be able to get close to her again. That thought was unthinkable. I was having so many doubts I was seriously thinking of changing my name to Thomas!

But something, or should I say, someone was telling me I should give it a try; after all, Eileen had put the suggestion in Helena's head as a way to make our connection stronger, so she was going to be there to answer my questions. I wanted so much to be as close as I possibly could to my girl, and if this was a way of doing that, then I could not afford to miss the opportunity.

So there I sat and thought about what my first question would be. It's funny because I always thought of so many questions that I would like to ask Eileen if I was given the chance, but when the time came, my mind went blank. I decided I needed to clear my head, so I sat quietly for a little while, trying to clear all the rubbish from my mind, and then the first question arrived:

"What is our mission together?"

I picked up the pen and waited, nothing for a few moments, then I heard in my mind, "Pick four cards", so I put down the pen, spread the cards out in front of me and picked the first card that caught my attention, then the next, the next and finally the last one. I turned them over to reveal 3. Becoming, 12. Peaceful Change, 44. Charity, and 21. Quiet Blossoming. I didn't really understand their meaning at that point, but I picked up the pen again and waited, trying to keep my mind still so I could be ready if a message came through or the pen started to move. Within a minute I got a message just sitting in my mind. Was this from Eileen, or was it just me imagining things? But the message was persistent, so I wrote it down:

> " We will write a book to help those who have lost loved ones. You will go in search of your inner self. I am always with you. We are one.

Then I asked if doing the circles with my Reiki teacher was beneficial for me, and once again I was asked to pick cards, this time just two, so I spread them out and picked 7. Answered Prayers, and 38. The Abundant Garden. This was quickly followed with:

> These are absolutely what you need to do. They will bring wisdom and satisfaction into your life.

I was overjoyed that we were once again talking, even if it had to be by using this method; this was so good.
Next question:

"What am I to you and you to me?"

Just one card was asked for: 36. With Moon At Feet. And the answer:

> As the moon and the earth are entwined by gravity, so are you and I.

Was I really having a conversation with my beautiful girl, my best mate and my lifelong companion? This was awesome; it was the best feeling that I had had for a very long time. Eileen was here; she was with me and there was the proof right in front of my eyes, in my scribbled writings. I wanted so much to keep talking, but my questions had come to an end, so I thought if I did some breathwork, maybe that would give me more inspiration. I went into the bedroom, lay on the bed, and started the breathwork, breathing through my nose, deep into my abdomen, then out through my mouth. This is quite exhausting if you are not used to doing it, and I only lasted a few minutes before I needed to rest. I lay there for a minute, then got up, went back to the table, picked up the pen, and before I could think of another question, Eileen said this to me:

> *I want you to know you are on the right path. You are always on the right path even when you think you are not. Oleb is with you, and I am guiding you, leading you as always. You are my light, and I am yours. The heat on your forehead—eternal love for you. Katie Melua song, remember it is true. Namasté.*

The date was the 24th of August 2018. It had been nineteen long months since my girl had left the Earth plane, nineteen long months of grappling with the grief that had shaken me to my very core, nineteen long months of searching and hoping that I could at least make some kind of connection with the one I so dearly loved, and now it was happening, in a way that I could never have imagined. My Eileen had guided me to those people who could help me on my path, enhancing my spiritual awareness and bringing me to this point in time when we were really connecting.

After the last answer, I had one more question:

"Who is Oleb?"

I picked two cards this time, which were 32. Gives Peace and 5. Soul Birth and waited, but this time there was no answer, just the cards for me to interpret.

From this day forward we regularly talked together in this way, and I realised that our wedding vows were not quite correct. We had said we would love and honour each other till death do us part, but death does not part us; we are still very much together, still loving and honouring each other, and will do so for eternity.

It didn't always turn out the way I hoped; there were occasions when I received no answer at all, and this was usually when I was allowing the grief to take over, for although I was so blessed to have this connection and with all the knowledge I had gained from Helena and the books I had read, even though I knew Eileen was with me I still felt the loss of her physical presence.

Sometimes I would just sit and write my thoughts down. One night when I was feeling particularly low, I said to her, "My life is so empty without you beside me in physical form. I drift from one day to the next without direction or purpose. It is as though my life has come to a standstill—waiting for the restart. You are my life, my love and my light, and until I can reconnect, I am in an abyss—a void. Please help me find the path that will lead me to a productive life and for us to make our connection so strong it will be as though you never left."

Although I didn't get a reply, I sensed she was around me. A few days later I asked her why we followed a healthy lifestyle if she was going to leave so early. By this time I was using my own cards; I was directed to pick three, which were Integrity, Peace and Chakra Balancing. Then came Eileen's reply:

> *"* We chose the healthy path to avoid the clutches of the medical industry. Choosing health gave us a better life. I needed to leave so you would be able to find your spirituality. It would never have happened if I were there. You needed a catalyst. The cards confirm the integrity of mind and body for the most part, and following the spiritual healing path, such as Reiki, will give peace of mind and a balancing of the whole body.

This seemed as though it was all for my benefit, but surely there had to be more than that; surely Eileen must have gained something from all this, it can't be all about me. After asking the question and picking three cards, Emotional Release, Automatic Writing, and Psychic Conversations, Eileen said:

> We work together as a team. My passing gave me a release from the stress of the last two years. We need to hone our skills of connection across the dimensions. The joy of life is in the journey.

It was often the case that once one question was answered, another would form in my mind. The following is a transcript of a series of conversations I had with Eileen during September 2018.

M: What happened when you left?

Cards: Messages, Meditation, Heart Mind Balance

E: *I wanted so much to tell you that I was OK. My stress and anxiety were gone, and that I was going home, but I really needed you to tune into me and I couldn't leave until this happened. I stayed around you, had to use the lorikeets to make the connection; you were so distraught. I didn't want to leave you; you did so well at the funeral. I had to leave part of my essence with you to try and comfort you. You must find your direction, have much to do.*

M: Do you have a message for Helena?

Cards: Past Lives, Oneness

E: *The many aspects of our being are interpreted in each life. We have been all kinds of races, and yet we are the one spirit from the one source. Probing past lives can help us understand that we are truly one; evolving as we are to higher levels and losing the fear of the unknown will make the Earth a better place. Namasté.*

M: Am I as different from others as I feel?

Cards: Finding A Mentor, Health, Heart Mind Balance

E: *The Universe is made up of many different species, and in each of those species, each individual is unique. To follow the path of the majority is not always the right path. Being different makes us question the status quo and form our opinions without being influenced by others. You are unique—not necessarily better or worse than others. Be proud of who you are, and remember you are still part of source like all others, but thrive in your individuality.*

M: Why do I feel so uncomfortable in social gatherings?

Cards: Automatic Writing, Kwan Yin, Oneness

E: *Although you know we are all part of the one source, you have a deep distrust of others, emanating from past lives. You need to see most others with more compassion and try to see the good in them. Your solitary lifestyles of the past make it difficult for you to socialise. Be with people you feel comfortable with and avoid the others. Remember, I too was a stranger at one time in this life, even if not for long.*

The optimal state of being is to be in spirit. We strive to evolve to the point where reincarnating is no longer necessary. In the meantime, we set ourselves "tests" on Earth to help us evolve. We need the differences, the opposites that occur on Earth, so we can experience them, and to experience something we don't like is to know what we do like. Even when someone comes into our life who causes us pain, they are teaching us; at the same time, they are also learning. All is well.

M: Who were you met by when you went home?

Cards: Friendship, Past Lives, The Threshold

> E: *Our group was there to meet me; you were in the background as you are still incarnating, those who played significant roles in this past life, my Mum especially and Jim (Eileen's brother). It is a wonderful thing to be back in spirit with all our friends. Win says take care—enjoy life, do the walk, and see if you can beat her stay.*

Win had been my aunt; she lived to the ripe old age of 103, so I think she was setting me a challenge! The walk she spoke of was suggested to me during one of my sessions with Helena, who asked me if I knew of the Camino de Santiago, a pilgrimage of around 800 km from the Pyrenees in France across Spain to the magnificent cathedral in Santiago de Compostela, where the remains of St. James (Santiago in Spanish) are said to be interred. She felt this would be a way for me to make a stronger connection with Eileen and all those others in spirit who are around me. I must admit I had never heard of it but was intrigued, so I did the usual thing we all do when we want to find out more: I searched "camino" on the internet and discovered an epic journey that is changing people's lives.

It is a pilgrimage that has been taken by many for hundreds of years, and the cathedral is a significant site for the Catholic religion. Modern-day pilgrims do it for many reasons; just to take time out from the constant bombardment of modern life with all its instant communication through mobile phones, emails, the Facebook syndrome, and all those other social media interactions and day-to-day stresses would be as good a reason as any, but many find a reawakening of their spirituality or religious beliefs whilst undertaking this pilgrimage.

The walk, which takes at least 32 days, allows the pilgrim, or "peregrino" as they are known in Spain, to experience the feeling of truly being at one with nature, to be able to feel the accomplishment of the body overcoming the rigour of walking an average of 25 km per day, to have the freedom to allow all those pent-up emotions to surface and be cleared, to be able to really get in touch with their innermost feelings, and for many, to feel a real connection with their God and expand their spirituality.

I knew that Eileen had sown this seed for me to nurture and grow, and this prompted me to ask my next question:

"Is the Camino going to be important and significant for me?"

Once again I got the message to pick cards, which I did: Soul Birth and Abundant Garden, and then Eileen answered:

> *"* You will connect with me in ways you can't imagine. It will be like a rebirth of our connection. You will see many wonderful things, and I will be with you every step of the way. You will feel my presence, our bond will become greater, and you will know the truth. The light is within you; it glows with a burning desire to seek the truth and to trust in the Universe.

I was convinced! I had to do this, I knew it would be a hugely significant step forward for me both mentally and spiritually, and the promise of a much stronger connection with my Eileen was the jewel in the crown. I did a lot more research and watched several videos of people who had completed the pilgrimage for all sorts of different reasons, yet whatever their reason for initially starting out, they all found this journey to be profoundly life-changing, giving them a new, positive, and less materialistic outlook on life.

If this sparks an interest in you to find out more, I can really recommend a book by the German comedian Hape Kerkeling, called "I'm Off Then", very aptly subtitled "Losing and finding myself on the Camino de Santiago", which is a frank and entertaining account of his journey along the Camino.

I told my daughter in America what I was planning to do, and she said she would like to come with me, so we decided we would go in

August of 2020, which would give us both enough time to do some training, both mentally and physically, to prepare for the reality of walking continuously for over six weeks across Spain.

Even though I had these goals now to focus on, I would still feel so very alone at times, but Eileen was always there to remind me she was with me. I asked her what I needed to do to try and cope with the situation, and after picking three cards, Personal Transformation, Meditation, and Passion, she said to me:

> " You know that I am with you always; I have never left you—only in physical form. Allow me to give you the strength. Go within and find bliss. The Camino will be the key; embrace it. See wonder in nature. Believe in yourself; you are not alone. Focus on that which you have and not that which you think you have lost. Take on life to the full; see the beauty in all around you. To see the beauty in a petal is to truly connect with spirit.

The phrase that caught my attention was, "*Focus on that which you have and not that which you **think** you have lost*". I had not lost her; she was closer to me than ever before, and she would keep reminding me of this whenever I faltered. I have this wonderful partner who was the love of my life whilst here on Earth and now is my spiritual guide and still the love of my life, who is always by my side. All I have to do is to BELIEVE without question that this is the truth.

I decided it was time to have some fun with her, so I asked what would be the winning lotto numbers for the next big draw on the Saturday. The cards were Self-Acceptance, Asking For Help and Prosperity, and the answer was what I was starting to expect from my girl—very profound and seeing past the base of the question. I knew she wouldn't give me the actual numbers, for that would be cheating!

> "You will choose the numbers if you are to win; your story has already been written. If it is to be, then so it will be. You have prosperity in your life in so many ways—that friendship with your two Reiki mates—gorgeous people. You have our beautiful family, and we have ourselves. There are many ways to be rich on Earth, and those things that money cannot buy are the most precious."

How true this is, for to have sufficient money can make life more comfortable and take some of the stresses away, but the real prosperity comes from those things that money simply cannot buy—good friendships, being at one with nature, and finding the peace within.

I followed up with some breathwork and received this beautiful message, which can give us all the peace of mind that when we physically die, we go to a wonderful place we all call home, and yet we can still be around those still incarnating.

> Beyond this realm there is a place filled with love and compassion. It is our real home where we can evolve as souls to higher levels, but many of us need the experience of the traumas and ecstasies of happenings on Earth to accelerate our evolution. Death as you know it is not an end; it is only a transition. We are immortal as souls, and our Earth paths lead us to higher levels of knowledge. Know that I am always by your side, whether it be in physical or spiritual form. Believe and trust this because it is THE TRUTH. The cycles of reincarnation enable us to experience the whole.

As Eileen was talking about reincarnation, I asked her if she could tell me anything about my past lives, for surely our past life experiences must affect our present thought patterns.

> "Your past lives are yours to discover; they are culminating in your present life. I cannot tell you the details; that will be for you to find out if it is to be so, but I can tell you we have always been together for millennia. We have a bond that will never be broken. It is said that all will be revealed when the time is right. You may find a time when regression will serve a purpose, but it is a deliberate act of amnesia that prevents you from knowing all that was in your other incarnations, for to know would cloud your perspective of this life and would lessen the learning.

There have been other times when Eileen has referred to my past lives, but the information is always very sketchy and never really gives me an idea of what took place. I can only assume that at this time, I am not supposed to know the details; as she said, maybe when the time is right, I will find out.

You may remember I talked about the book Helena was thinking of about the man who went in search of a connection to his wife who had passed. After I started doing these writings with Eileen, I would always take what we had written to my sessions with Helena, and it was interesting how often she would be talking to me before she had seen them about a particular subject that Eileen had already talked about and was in the writings. She said that the book she had seen was the book I was going to write, and these conversations I was having with Eileen would be a significant part of it. She told me the book would bring reassurance to those who think they have lost a loved one—that those loved ones are still around them.

I must admit I was very doubtful I would be able to do this. I was no one special; who was I to give people the hope they were looking for? But I did have this very special connection with my girl, and I knew without any doubt that she was always with me. There was the proof right in front of my eyes in the exercise books filled with information that certainly couldn't have come from me, for sometimes I needed Helena to explain Eileen's answers before I could properly understand them.

I had no idea how I would go about doing this, so I asked the question and received this answer:

> The words will flow when you are ready; do not rush. Piecing together the facts is time-consuming. The message will be one of hope. Write as it comes to you, then assemble it into order. Don't try too hard; remember we are writing this together, I will help you when you need it. Your first book has inspired another to follow suit; take heart from that, and this will be even more inspirational. Words will come at the right time; your new experiences and the Camino are tools you will use. Together we will inspire and bring peace to many.

The first book Eileen talked about was a photo book I put together about her life and our life together; it is filled with wonderful memories combining photos and my thoughts. This was really good therapy for me, as I was able to focus on the amazing life we had together rather than my grief; it brought me great joy to be able to remember the good times we had and is a beautiful record for my children and grandchildren to have. I have shown it to my family and friends; they all thought it was such a good idea and a fitting tribute to Eileen. My neighbour was so impressed that she wanted to make her own book of a very special trip to New Zealand she had done and asked me to help her with it; I was only too pleased to help.

November 2018 was closing in, so I thought it timely to ask Eileen which horse would win the Melbourne Cup, which is the most famous race on the horse racing calendar here. She knows I don't bet, so I thought maybe she would tell me, and she did, but as usual, it was a metaphorical answer that meant nothing to me at the time:

> "The race of kings is always won by the king of the race. Interminable. Wait and see.

As it turned out, the race was won by a horse called Cross Counter, owned by a company whose founder is His Highness Sheikh Mohammed bin Rashid Al Maktoum from Dubai. The answer was there if I had known anything about racing, but then if I had, Eileen probably wouldn't have told me or would have made her answer even more obscure. Pretty amazing though, she is so smart, and I just love her to bits.

I was thinking that with all my questions, perhaps I was taking up too much of her time and not letting her concentrate on her spiritual agenda, so once again I asked her. The two cards I picked were Warrior and Happiness, and her answer has a message that everyone should hear:

> "We are all here to help, but this will happen differently at different times. I am always with you; time is not taken up as there is no linear time in spirit. I am with you just as I am with our children, even though our youngest doesn't feel me. Your guide is guiding you, and with his help, I am too; you can ask for help from any one of us. You have to remember, we in spirit are multitaskers, as you would say, and do many things simultaneously. Never feel you are a burden; we are kindred spirits—to help each other when in need. You have done this for me in previous incarnations.
>
> We would ask you to cast aside doubts and fears and worries, and strive for happiness with the knowledge that we are always with you.

Know that your loved ones in spirit, along with your guides and other members of your spiritual group, are always ready and willing to listen and help, but if you don't ask, they cannot help, so it is important to reach out to make a strong connection.

The more I talk to Eileen, the more I know our connection is real. I ask her all kinds of questions, from personal ones to questions about life in the spirit world and just about everything in between. For quite a while, I was never sure whether the thoughts were mine or Eileen's when I was writing them down, but after reading them back, there was no doubt, for many of the answers are so profound I know they are not from me. I would often have a preconceived idea of what the answer may be, but when the answer came, it was generally not what I had imagined, and Eileen would almost always have good advice for me.

With Eileen watching me progress in this life, I wondered whether it was frustrating for her to see me allowing situations to get the better of me. She said:

> Frustration is not an emotion we have in spirit; it is the human traits and emotions that cause you to be swayed by your situations. You need to view it as if it were on a movie screen. Take a step back and use logic to analyse any situation. I do not feel frustration, but I do feel sad for you that you cannot rise above it, although having incarnated on Earth, I do understand. Seek the bliss in your life and you will find me.

I was asking questions regularly because it made Eileen feel so much closer to me, and I was always inspired by her answers. My questions in November and December of 2018 covered all sorts of topics:

M: Do you miss this beautiful country?

Cards: Life Journey, Finding A Mentor, Acceptance

E: *There are many beautiful places on Earth; nature at its best is truly awesome. You are lucky to live in a part of the world that has so much beauty—though luck really does not have a part in it. In spirit we can recreate beautiful places we visited on Earth; to miss is not the right expression, as in spirit we have wonderful places too. The physical content that is the Earth does make the feeling different, but life can be wonderful whether we are there on Earth or here in spirit; it is all a matter of perspective.*

Remember to appreciate all that nature has to offer; when you are immersed in nature, you are close to source energy. The Earth can be a powerful teacher if you are open to learning its lessons.

M: I understand that life on Earth is about experiencing contrasts, but why do the contrasts seem to favour the dark side? People are trying to con us at every turn, and there is still so much violence and hatred in the world?

Cards: The Threshold, Love

E: *It is in the eye of the beholder. It is true that there is a lot of dark activity on Earth, but there is also a building of the light. Those on the dark side are struggling to maintain their grip on Earth's societies; they know this energy that is new will eventually envelop them, and this is their way of resisting.*

There is so much good in the world, but it often goes unnoticed as it is not "news worthy". This will change as the energy increases, and people will start wanting to shun those from the dark, so more light will come into this world.

It is important to have contrasts—night and day, hot and cold—so we can find what we like and what we do not. We all grow from our experiences; they grow our souls, whether they be considered good or bad.

Connecting Through Writing

Look for the light in your world and shun the darkness; it will self-destruct. Appreciate all that is good in your life and focus on those things that make you feel good. Remember, the better you feel about yourself, the better your connection to source, which is always Light. You must try to overcome the situations that are dragging you down; ask us for help and support. We are always ready to help but do not put limitations on how we may do this; there are more ways for us to help than you can imagine, and if you limit the possibilities to what you believe, you will be blocking the energy.

There are no accidents, everything is done for a reason, and it all comes back to the growth of our souls.

Please TRUST in this, my dearest, and know we are still together, if not both in physical; in fact, I can be closer to you more often now than I could be before.

M: Do we decide when we are born astrologically so our personality matches?

Card: Four Of Earth

E: *Nothing is an accident; all aspects of your future personality will be taken into consideration. Astrological data is imprinted on your human mind, and birth time is defined by these traits. There are many different perspectives in each astrological sign depending on the placement of the planets at the time of birth; it is a carefully chosen decision when you will be born. For example, no two Geminis are the same, as there are many variables that make up their personalities. Each and every one of you is unique, and may we all be blessed for that.*

Sometimes I have no question but still sit with pen in hand to see if Eileen has a message for me, and when she does, it is always pertinent to my circumstances. She always encourages me to continue with our writings.

> "You must continue to write this way if you are to increase your connection with me. It is important that you don't lose faith in this; you are doing well, but you will have setbacks from time to time. This is because your focus is not fully here. You are seeing all the negative sides of situations, which causes blockages. Be proud you have made such a good connection in such a short time, while many never achieve this level.
>
> We are always together; you MUST BELIEVE THIS. Cast your doubts aside and really try to focus on the positives. I know this is hard for you, as you have always seen the dark side of things, but there is so much light around you—embrace it.
>
> The more you have a positive attitude and your spirit is high, the better our connection. Be happy with where we are at the moment, be grateful you and I are so close, and know that our connection can only grow more powerful with your positivity and happiness.
>
> With the upcoming festive season, you may need to take a quiet approach; it is always hard for you at this time of the year, as you are not enamoured with the Christmas spirit. Forget the commercialisation and focus more on the spiritual aspects of the time. See the good in people and try to understand that socialising is an opportunity to get to know people. You analyse too much; take things more on their face value.
>
> Remember, I am always with you; don't expect too much too soon, it will come in time, and then you will see the beauty in all things good, and good things will come to you.

More breathwork:

" When storm clouds build and the storm comes closer, lightning flashes and thunder roars. Even at its darkest moment as the lightning strikes, the air is energised, the pouring rain nourishes the earth with nutrients provided to enhance the growth of living things. Ionised air clears away the mist, and when the storm has passed, everything can be seen clearer, crisp and clean as though it has been rejuvenated.

Look for the lightning that will clear the air around you and enhance your vision, both internally and externally. Appreciate the rain as it washes away the dust and leaves everything fresh and clean. Sunshine then brings in the light to complete the cycle. Remember life is a series of cycles; when we go through times we think are bad, there is always that lightning strike to clear the air and give us a better vision and understanding of our circumstances. Nothing is totally light or dark; one complements the other. See the beauty in all things and try to see the purpose behind the situation. Find enjoyment in life; it is not the scene that confronts you, it is how you react to that scene. Seek the joy and be grateful.

Now pick a card:

Card: Automatic Writing

" You will become more fluent at this the more you practice. Writing together is good for both of us; for you it helps you feel our connection, for me it is a great way to communicate. Nothing is better than for us to be together this way at this time.

Around this time, the sessions with Helena would get put back for various reasons; something would come up, and we would have to reschedule. I really looked forward to the sessions and was disappointed when they were cancelled, but I figured there must be a reason, so I posed the question to Eileen, and as usual, she was telling me to accept the situation and look for the benefits in it.

> The time is right when the time is right. It is not the physical date that is important, but more the timing of the event. Perhaps you need to experience something before the meeting. Nothing happens by accident; there is always a reason why things happen when they do. Go with the flow and let the flow carry you downstream; apparent delays will be beneficial in the long term.

We as humans see everything from our own perspective, and we often have difficulty seeing others' points of view. If we can understand that all situations can be viewed from different standpoints, then we may have a better understanding of those situations as a whole and be able to accept that our perspective is not the only possibility. Eileen has often emphasised this in our talks. After doing some breathwork, I received this little gem:

> As a new day breaks, it is as though it is a new beginning; yet it is all a part of the cycle of life on Earth. Sunrise is only a perspective from which you see as a resident of Earth; yet the sun doesn't rise—the perception of a rising sun is put in motion by the Earth spinning on its axis. The Earth is what is actually moving. Perception is in the mind of the beholder; many things we take for granted, such as the sunrise and set, are not what they seem to be; it is all a matter of your viewpoint. The Moon seems much larger when low in the sky than when it is high in the sky, yet it is not.
>
> The same can be said about life and death; they are not the start and end but parts of an eternal cycle of growth for our souls. Though you cannot see me, I am still with you always; the secret

is BELIEVING. Believe and it will be; not everything appears as it really is. Trust, and all will be well. Be happy, and happiness will surround you.

I just love how she regularly lets me know that, although I cannot feel or see her, she is around me. My perspective would have me believe that she isn't, but I have seen past that and now know without a doubt that she is here. They say that seeing is believing, but if we believe absolutely, then we can believe without seeing.

By January 2019, I had started on the book but was unsure whether what I was writing was on the right track. It was close to the second anniversary of Eileen's departure from this Earth, and I was going through a lot of mixed emotions. Eileen had another message for me:

> Our connection can only grow strong when you fill your heart with joy, not trepidation. Let go of your worries, as they solve nothing. Remember what you told me in those last two years. Seek the joy in life, know that all situations are there for you to learn from, look back at those that caused you grief, and try to learn from them. It is time for you to move forward and put the past behind.
>
> Your book will come about over time; you have made a start, but take it slowly—allow the thoughts to come; if they don't, don't force them, just let it flow. You need to read 'Conversations With God', it will help you realise our connection is real. I am always by your side. Keep trying to move ahead.

Then she asked me to pick a card, and I picked Trust. It never ceases to amaze me how the right card turns up at the right time, for to trust completely is to believe completely, and if we can do this, our loved ones in spirit can be with us. The more we trust and believe, the more signs they are with us will appear, and the more we will recognise them. I took Eileen's advice and bought a copy of "Conversations With God" by Neale Walsh and randomly opened it to the page where Neale was asking how he could know he was actually communicating with God and it was not just his imagination, something I was often wondering when I was talking to Eileen. The answer was that communication from God can come in all forms, through our thoughts, imagination, or other ways when necessary. This is also the case when communicating with anyone in spirit.

On January 16th, 2019, two years since Eileen made her transition, I did some breathwork, and she said:

> " Many aspects of your life have changed since I came home; you have found spirituality you would not have, had I still been in physical. I have guided you to find the Reiki teacher so you could experience the energies of Reiki, and you have completed two levels—all that you need. Your Reiki has helped those you have performed it on even if you don't see the benefits. I have guided you to Helena through Jasmine so you will have a better understanding of the way things really are. Your grief has held you back a little, but you are doing well. Remember, as always, I am always by your side; look for the signs—you picked up on the feather, but there are many others that you have missed.
>
> To move forward is to believe, and to understand this life of yours is just a part of the journey, nonetheless a very important part, and it is in your interest to follow the paths that bring you happiness. The fact that today is the second anniversary of my passing; see it as a milestone you have achieved, and look back over the period to realise how you have advanced spiritually. I have great faith that you will achieve your necessary goals, and obstacles that come your way will be overcome. You will do the walk, and your feet will carry you the distance. Have faith in yourself, be kind to yourself. All is well. I love you.

I kept talking to her on a regular basis, usually two or three times a week. If I didn't have specific questions, I would do some breathwork and see whether I would get a message. The information I get is always very profound and full of wisdom:

> There comes a time in everyone's life when they need to truly find themselves. This may take the form of meditation retreats, but it can also be just by getting into nature. For others, the process may be more complicated, and that is how it is with you. My passing gave you the impetus to seek out your truth, and you are being guided to those who can help you the most.
>
> There are many facets to the process, and if you embrace them all, you will truly discover yourself. You need a balance between everyday life and the search for your true identity. You are progressing well but don't focus solely on the soul; the physical is as important. With these sessions we have together, allow them to come when they are ready, don't try to force them, the more you allow, the more information I can pass on to you.
>
> Remember, to enjoy your time on Earth for to enjoy is to enhance your experience, both physically and spiritually. Happiness and growth of the soul are intertwined.

I just love to talk to her this way because I feel so much closer to her when I do, and am often amazed at the answers she gives.

M: Can you tell me something I would have to look up to verify?

Cards: Ascended Masters, Personal Transformation

E: *All the knowledge in the Universe is there for anyone who wishes to access it. There are no thoughts that haven't been thought before; although it may seem that technology is producing new concepts, the technology is just utilising what is and always has been, but in a different way.*

Because in spirit there is no future or past; all those ideas that seem new and innovative have always been. Those who appear to have the new ideas are just locking into the already existing concept—they are tuning in. Source is all-knowing, and it is when you access Source that the inspiration occurs. Inspiration literally means from spirit (Source). Seek the Source and seek the light, and you too can be inspired. Meditation will help you.

M: Wasn't today great! The session with Helena in the morning, then Reiki and food with my two Reiki mates.

Cards: Heart Mind Balance, Prosperity

E: *It was good to see you enjoying yourself at last. Amy and Ruth make a great combination with you; your differences seem wide apart, but in fact they are not as far apart as you might imagine. The three of you complement each other, each with his/her own slant on things. I love to see the three of you performing spiritual healing on each other; the energy is intense. And I am so happy that you have been able to continue the friendship from where I physically left off—you realise it really is now a quartet.*

And your session with Helena; she reiterates what I have been telling you—so very wise she is. We are kindred spirits, she and I, and it is always good to work with her.

Remember today as the starting point for you to move forward; keep the joy in your life, and the joy will be with the both of us. Blessings be with you always, and as always I am by your side, here to encourage. Know that you are never alone;

we are always together across the dimensions.

M: How do I get the mindset to do meditation and stay healthy?

Cards: Nature Journey, Rewards

E: *It is hard for many to clear their minds for meditation; limiting your focus to breathing or the flame of a candle can help quieten the constant chatter that our brains output. It is an individual process for each person; the candle may work for some but not for others, likewise the breathing focus. You must try different approaches and find the one that quietens the mind the most, then concentrate on that one. When the mind is quieted, visualise yourself in perfect health, walking through meadows filled with flowers or walking along a beach with the waves lapping at your feet; tranquillity is the key.*

Take this a step further, and turn the visualisation into your reality. Go for that walk in the meadow or along the beach; be in awe of the wonderment of nature, the colours, the textures, and the detail. Seek out the stars at night and see that small part of the Universe that is your focus. Understand that what you see is from your perspective; others may see it differently. The Universe is a wonderful place with so much to offer and so many dimensions to choose from, and yet it is all one source, as we all are; everything is interconnected and intertwined. Your perspective gives you the appearance of separation because your focus as a human is narrow.

This is a wonderful thing, this Universe of yours, coupled with all the other universes that make the whole. Embrace this all and appreciate it. Give thanks that you are a part of such a wonderful experience and be joyful—health will follow.

M: How can I make a difference when the collective consciousness of the world seems to be bent on destroying it?

Cards: Health, Opportunity

E: *Live life with joy; the more joyous you make life, the healthier you will be in body, mind and spirit. Go to Helena's session with an open heart and allow the Universe to unfold before you. The wisdom of the Universe is at your disposal; all you have to do is to hear it.*

You are a magnificent being like us all, and we are all part of Source or God, whatever you want to call it. Know this and know you are worthy; believe this, and wonderful things and events will fill your life. You are getting an idea of God's intentions for us all, especially while we are on the Earth's plane. Try to understand what he says in the book, for she is giving you the truth.

I will be with you as I always am when you see Helena; we all will be there to nurture and encourage you. Have faith in yourself, and you will do magnificent things; you are more powerful than you think.

M: How can I help others make the connection like we have as quickly as we did?

Card: Love

E: *Unfold our lives together, both before and after I returned home. We were lucky that we had left formal religions behind to find spirituality; this released the limitations of what we perceived of what is. You gave me your blessing to return home, which made it easier for us to rejoin. Your grief stood in the way for a while, but you had an underlying belief that I was still around you; that made it easier for me to make the connection, even if it was through the lorikeets to start with. You kept searching, and I guided you to those who could serve us best for our connection. The key is to BELIEVE.*

This can be difficult for those with the shackles of religion, but if they try and have the KNOWING that we are not gone, just transitioned to spirit, and that we are always with our loved ones who remain on Earth, including that part of them that is in spirit with us. The power of true love is the most powerful energy and can overcome all obstacles. LOVE and BELIEVE; with these two qualities the connection will happen.

M: Why do we have incidents that can frustrate us?

Cards: Peace, Blessings

E: *All situations are presented to you for your growth. Different people's lives become entwined in the situation but for different reasons for each person. You have heard before that it isn't the situation that presents itself; it is the way you react to that situation. Those whose lives have been entwined by the same situation can learn from each other's reactions. It may be the other reacts in a way you should have, or vice versa. It is all about learning; when you see the reaction of the other and think it is a good one, then look at your response. There is no right or wrong way because all is in the learning, even if it is to learn that you don't want to react in such a way. To know how not to react is to know how to react. Black and white, light and dark—it is all about the contrasts that make you who you are.*

M: I have never seemed to have taken what I am told for granted—questioning and forming my own opinions. Is that what makes me feel different from most others? Am I self-creating?

Cards: Emotional Release, Community

E: *You have lived many lives, and although the amnesia prevents you from knowing the details, you have an inner knowing. If you are told the "common truths" and they don't ring true, it is because you are tapping into this inner knowing.*

Your experiences from past lives have taught you not to trust everything you are told, so you look for facts to back up these "truths". It is good to question, especially when the knowledge offered does not make sense to you. It is often your higher self that is doing the questioning; there is a wealth of underlying knowledge accumulated from past lives and in spirit. I reiterate, there are no new thoughts; all has been thought before, but others may try to bend these thoughts to suit their purposes. Look to your intuition (for that comes from spirit) for guidance; listen to that gut feeling, and you will never be a sheep.

Breathwork:

It is a wonderful thing we do, you and I, for we have an unbreakable bond, and together we will bring the light to those who believe they have lost a loved one. Those who truly seek the truth will find us and will be comforted by what they discover, for they already know the truth of life and death; they just need to remember.

M: Is all sickness thought-provoked, or does some occur, like a pinched nerve, as purely a physical problem?

Cards: Acceptance, Meditation

E: *Sickness is often a state of mind. You do not consciously bring in a particular disease, but your emotions and level of self-worth can play a part in your overall health. Knowing this allows you to reverse dis-ease by bringing your mindset back to joy. If you are joyful and at ease with yourself, then you cannot have dis-ease. Believing in yourself can go a long way towards good health. The physical aspects may seem like a mechanical function, but you always have the power to be healthy. It is easier for you to see the so-called practical physical ailment as a misalignment of your body in the case of a pinched nerve, and the practitioner who "corrects" this only does so because you believe it is possible.*

A healthy lifestyle, good foods and nutrition, are always the best path, as if you follow these protocols with the absolute belief they will keep you healthy, then it will be. That is not to say eating non-foods will do the same, as the physical body requires proper nourishment for optimal health.

Be joyful and you will be healthy, but be truly joyful, from the heart.

I wasn't always able to connect with Eileen; sometimes I would try and get no response for a few days, and this would make me start to doubt our connection, but the next time we talked, she would often give me encouragement and tell me to just allow the process to take place. One time after I had tried without success for several days, she came through without my asking a question and said:

> When the time is right the words will flow, allow the words to evolve in your mind, just let it be. Trying to force progress will create resistance and will be detrimental to your growth.

Patience and trust and to truly believe are the keys.

This was just what I needed to hear, because I am not the most patient person in the world, to say the least! I am always wanting to make our connection stronger, but it can be frustrating when we have had a good run of questions and answers and I am feeling really connected to her to suddenly find it isn't happening. When I look at those times, it is usually because my mind is being sabotaged by thoughts induced by outside influences and incidents that have occurred during the day, and I am not clearing my mind.

So when I was going through a period where I was not connecting, I would try to clear my mind and just allow whatever came to me to come, and if there was nothing, to accept that and try again later. Generally, in a couple of days we would make our connection again and the words would start flowing, and that always made me feel so good. I still struggled with the fact that Eileen was no longer physically with me, and although our talks were proof positive that she was with me in spirit, at times I would really feel down. After one such occasion, I did some breathwork, and she gave me this message of encouragement that really lifted my spirits:

> " Weep not for me, for I am in a place of contentment now. You did all you could for me, and I thank you for that. Know the outcome was always as it would be; it is our story that we continue our journey in different dimensions, but together. You are my eyes and my ears in the physical. Through you I experience your life and times, so be joyful so we can be joyful together. You are not alone, you know this, and you must believe this. I am with you always, or I would not be able to experience life on Earth at this present time. You and I have a partnership in this period of your life on Earth.
>
> I will help guide you to your best experiences, and in return I will feel the joy you feel, taste the foods that you eat, and suffer

your sorrows. So make this a joyous time; forget what might have been because it would never have been. You know our stories were written before incarnating—we have a lot of evolving; for me spiritually and for you both physically and spiritually. You have done so well; setbacks will come and go, just allow them and then move forward.

I have no regrets, and neither should you, for it is all in the experience; it is how we progress on our path to divinity. I love you and know you love me. Keep pushing for the love and cast aside the fear. We are one.

My questions kept coming, and during March we covered some interesting topics. I was wondering what it was about mediums that gave them the ability to connect so well with those in spirit. Was it a special talent they had or could anyone do it? Eileen always gave me answers that made so much sense.

M: Are mediums more open to connections? Is that why they can act as a go-between?

Cards: Meditation, Wisdom

E: *Everyone has the ability to receive their guides and loved ones from spirit, but the mediums set themselves back and allow the energies to flow. They are impartial conveyors of information, although they can put their personality into the flow of information. Those who do not consider themselves mediums generally have vested interests in the information they want to receive, and because of this, put up barriers and blockages.*

You all can channel the information, but many have preconceived ideas of what should be said, and this blocks us from delivering our messages. You have the information within you, and mediums are able to lock into that and release it to you.

Channelling is a matter of allowing the information to flow without input from yourself—you are doing this right now, yet you would not consider yourself a medium. Mediums have the ability to be impartial observers and to interpret the energies they receive, which makes it easier for us to connect.

M: Is the purpose of our lives to find out who we are, are we learning or remembering?

Cards: Prosperity, Oneness

E: *Part of our journey on Earth is to experience the contrasts, and our choices about those contrasts determine who we are at that time. As we evolve, those choices may change, and we will begin to see things for what they really are. It is both a learning and a remembering.*

M: What is the best way for those who have lost loved ones to re-connect with them?

Cards: Community, Life Journey

E: *The key to reconnecting is BELIEF. Those who truly believe will connect with their loved ones, for it is through believing that the mind will reach out and be open. There should be no limitations put on how we will connect with those on Earth, as there are myriads of possibilities. If you truly believe and are open to all possibilities, then it will be so. Jasmine has told of some of the ways we touch you, through the caress of the hair, feathers, birds, and even songs with meanings specific to you. Questions may be answered in articles you read, and thoughts may come to you as if out of the blue.*

    We are always around our loved ones, but they must reach

out for us to make contact. Love is with you always.

I was still seeing Irene every month or so, and we were both pleased with my progress, as the grief was no longer overwhelming me, and I felt I was coming to terms with my situation and getting used to my new relationship with Eileen. I knew she was always with me, the events of the past few days had certainly proved that to me. I told Irene about our writings and the information Eileen was giving me and how she was encouraging me and reinforcing my belief that she was here. At one session, she asked me to ask if Eileen was with her at times, because at the beginning of each session, she would always ask for guidance, and she sometimes felt Eileen's presence. So that night I put the question. Here is the answer I got:

❝ You have formed a close bond with Irene over the past few years, and you both enjoy each other's company, especially when delving into your mind. She gets as much out of your sessions as you do; she was very kind to me and did all in her power to help me, and although it may not have seemed so at the time, she was a great support to me. I love seeing you develop friendships with Irene and Helena. These beautiful smart women provide you with knowledge, which is invaluable to you.

You know I am with you always, so I am with you when you visit Irene, but because of the bond you have, I drop in from time to time. Irene's session with the medium was an opportunity I couldn't resist; I had to appear to her in a form she would recognise. As you know, I work with Helena, and we have had some interesting times. Together, these are important people in your life, and so they are also important to me. The pieces of the journey are starting to fall into place for you. To have such support is precious, and I love being on this journey with you. Many blessings to all.

Even after all this time and with the knowing and the proof that Eileen was with me, I still would feel very alone at times, often when the day's work was done and I had come to a loose end. It really didn't make sense to me that I could still feel this way considering what I now knew, but I did and wanted to know why, so once again I asked Eileen, my amazing partner who seems to have this wonderful ability to give me just the answer I need to hear, even if it isn't what I expected. Here is her answer, along with a couple more from questions asked over the following few days.

M: Why do I still feel so lonely at times, even though I know you are with me?

Cards: Rewards, Friendship

E: *You have not yet adapted to our new relationship; you still yearn for the physical aspect of me. It will take time and is something you will never totally achieve until you join me here in spirit. As humans, we crave the physical aspects of our relationships, and it is difficult to adjust to the physical-nonphysical connection. We need tangibility. I constantly give signs of my presence, but many of them you miss. That is not surprising because some are subtle and you are not tuning into them. You know our connection is strong, or we would not be doing this, and as we do this, you feel the connection. But when you fall into a state that does not align, you feel you have lost the connection and feel alone.*

The best way to feel connected and sense my presence is to be joyful, for being joyful is to be closer to Source, and being close to Source makes you close to me. I will always be with you whether you feel it or not; you and I are inseparable. Have faith and BELIEVE and know absolutely. As this part of your journey unfolds, you will realise the strength of our bond. This you already know; you just have to remember.

Whenever you have doubts and feel separated from me, revisit your journey since my transition to non-physical. Remind yourself of the synchronicities that have taken place to guide you to those who have become important in your life, and be joyful of the path you are on. You have much to do, and life will continue to be fulfilling for you; we have so much to do together, and every step will be a progression in the evolvement of our souls. Our love is strong—this is the emotion you need to nurture, and miracles will continue to happen for us. We are beautiful spirits entwined for eternity. Believe and be happy.

M: Why do we usually forget our dreams?

E: *The dreams you do remember are generally insignificant fragments of your imagination that are conjured from the previous day's events. You will remember some dreams because they bring you important messages, but many times in a proverbial state. Dreams not remembered are those that are from deep sleep; when you are in deep sleep and dreaming, you have come home. The events that take place are from a different dimension and source applies an amnesia to prevent confusion. You will only remember the dreams that are important to you at the time if they are from deep sleep.*

M: It's your birthday today; you would have been seventy, we should have been celebrating.

E: *Every day on Earth should be a celebration—a celebration of life and of gratitude. Today was and is a significant date for both of us, as it was the day I entered the Earth's realm and my last incarnation began. This was the start of an amazing journey that we would take together in the physical, and it should be re-*

membered for that. The fact that I am no longer in physical does not mean there should be sadness. Give thanks for the physical journey we both have enjoyed, and have the knowing that our journey continues. Be not sad, for this day is the anniversary of the catalyst that ensured our coming together in physical for this incarnation. Look back and be grateful for all we shared together, look forward and be grateful for all that is to come.

A short while after, I had been listening to songs sung by Karen Carpenter, who had tragically died from the effects of anorexia at the age of 32, and I had thought what a waste it was that such a talent was cut short. I asked Eileen why this sort of thing had to happen.

" If we remembered the anguish, sorrow and grief that follow a loved one's death from past lives, we would never enter into loving relationships in this life; that is one of the reasons we have the amnesia that blocks our past life experiences. When a loved one returns home, we should remember the joyful experiences and times we had with them. The death of everyone always brings meaning to some who are left behind; sometimes there are messages that come, which can be beneficial for mankind as a whole. At other times there will be an awakening for just one or two of those left behind; no one dies without a learning taking place.

You thought earlier about Karen Carpenter while you were listening to her singing; you thought it was such a waste, but was it? Karen's soul came into that life and followed the journey she had chosen. Since her death, there has been a global awakening of the problems associated with the disease you call anorexia. From her death, more understanding has come about regarding the cause and effects of this imbalance of the mind, and much has been achieved in the treatment. No life is wasted even if it seems it is cut short; there is always a lesson to be remembered. So try not to hold on to grief; be happy for the soul, for they have fulfilled their goals and have returned home.

Our journey as souls is a combination of incarnations and being in spirit. It is a cycle in which, as we progress, so does the advancement of our soul, and as each and every soul develops, so it is beneficial to Source. Nothing is without reason; there is a purpose in everything, every situation, and everyone. As we evolve, either on Earth or in spirit, so does our collective energy grow. As previously stated, without the forced amnesia before reincarnation, we would not love, as we would fear the separation of a loved one at the time of death, and yet we all know in our hearts that we never lose loved ones; they—we—are always with you and are closer than ever before in this incarnation. You can't get rid of us that easily!

My love is always with you as yours is with me. Blessings.

This reminded me of the Carpenters song "We've Only Just Begun", which was released in 1970 and seemed particularly significant as our married journey had only just begun at that time. I often asked Eileen if she had a message for me before I went to see Helena, and this time she answered with a reference to that song.

" The Carpenters' song "We've Only Just Begun" resonated with us when we first got married, and now that our new relationship has only just begun, we are on an amazing journey together, and Helena is guiding you along your course. We have many adventures to participate in, and you and I will enjoy new experiences together. As the world unfolds before you, you will gain greater insights into what we are really on Earth for and an understanding of our soul's purpose. Past lives may become important to you, and if they do, they will be revealed. Don't push for information when you may not be ready for it; just go with the flow of events and allow the Universe to provide you with the knowledge when you are ready. Take one step at a time and don't rush; you are on course and on time and should be savouring every moment of it.

Our strength is in our knowing that we are always together. Remember this and be joyful.

As June 2019 arrived, my thoughts turned to our wedding anniversary, which was on the 6th. On that day I wished Eileen a happy anniversary whilst sitting with pen in hand, and she replied with this beautiful message:

> My blessings and best wishes are with you always, but today is special, for it is the 49th anniversary of our truly coming together in this life. 49 years ago we pledged our vows to one another, and over those years we have adhered to those pledges. Today is a celebration of that start to our married life, and regardless of other earthly events that surround you at present, it is a milestone we can both be proud of. We have been together for millennia and have shared many lives together in all sorts of relationships, but in this last incarnation, the one you are presently living, our partnership has been the closest and most rewarding; the proof of that is in the fact we are still in partnership and totally connected, even though I am in spirit and you are on Earth.
>
> Our love is deep and eternal; it is the greatest gift we can give each other.
>
> Celebrate every day, for each day is another day we share together. We are together and shall be forever. My love is yours, and yours is mine. It is indestructible. We are one.

As we travel through life, we encounter periods of great stress and upheaval at times. We meet people we wish we hadn't, and we often find ourselves questioning our abilities during these trying times. If you listen to channels such as Abraham, they will tell you that we are all here to seek the joy in life and live it to the fullest, but sometimes that is not so easy to do from our earthly perspectives. I asked Eileen why we had to have stressful events in our lives. She told me to pick two cards—Opportunity and Openness—then, through my thoughts, she said these words that could just as easily apply to anyone as well as me:

> These are all part of the contrasts we have come to Earth to experience. Stressful or even frightening events often occur to prod us into taking some kind of action; it may be to be aware of a possible situation, or it may be to help change our course. We have the contrasts of stresses and moments of pure joy, which are all experiences that promote soul growth if we react to them in a positive way. They are learning experiences that we undertake to provide us with the experience of the contrasts that are all around us when on Earth. To live a life without contrasts would be to slow our progress as souls, but don't think that because you have reacted in a way that you feel is unworthy, that you have not learnt from it.
>
> There is no situation that is presented to you that your soul is not aware of, even if the reason for that situation presenting is obscure to you. We are all here beside you and encouraging you to excel, but it is for you to take up the challenge. I know you are struggling with my lack of physicality, but be strong, and we will be strong together. I am with you always and love you as you love me. Blessings and namasté.

I must admit that at the time I was not feeling very strong. My emotions were often getting the better of me, especially in stressful situations. Eileen told me to pick another two cards, which were Prosperity and Appreciation, and continued:

> Grief can take many forms and produce a variety of emotions. For some there is anger, for others just a complete sense of loss, but there are many other stages in between. For you, your emotions have become raw, and you find it difficult to control the sadness that overwhelms you at times. The least thing can set you off, and you become overcritical of yourself. You are far too hard on yourself. You must be kind to yourself, for you have a good heart. To say you are weak is not to recognise your strengths.
>
> Together we were such a strong team because we supported each other in all our endeavours and adversities. You were of such incredible strength to me during those stressful times I went through, especially in those last two years. Your strength was what made all the difference, but it is not just your strength; it is also your compassion that carried me through those trying times.
>
> You must understand that all of us make mistakes during our lives; this is how we learn, and you are no different. Again, this is all about contrasts; from mistakes we learn what not to do, and as such, learn what we should do. You lack an appreciation of your talents, your kindness, and your good heart. See yourself as the magnificent being that you are, and recognise those positive aspects that make you who you are.
>
> So don't be down on yourself when you err, for to err is to be human, and at this stage, human is mainly what you are in physical. Your higher self—that part of you that is in spirit—is, along with all of your family in spirit, always with you and cheering you on in this act of play we call life.
>
> You are doing all right, just lose the negatives and bring in the positives.

Her words of encouragement are always there for me. I know she is my ally and my confidant, just as she had been when in physical, and now she has the wisdom of the Universe at her behest. I talk constantly to her in my mind and sometimes I hear answers without the need for pen and paper, but we are not always talking about the deeper aspects of life.

You know how there are some people you simply don't want to be around or who are being difficult just for the sake of it. Eileen and others in spirit will tell us that they are a reflection of a part of ourselves that we need to pay attention to, but wouldn't it be nice if we could just scare them off!

So I asked Eileen "Can you haunt people? If so can I give you a couple of names?!!"

As always, her answer gave me food for thought.

> The definition of "haunting" is when someone in spirit makes their presence felt to another in physical, so in that case, I must be haunting you!
>
> Haunting in the theatrical sense is not what we do, for we are not in the habit of scaring someone out of their wits. We always come with love and affection. To haunt someone in the way you ask is to try to coerce them into different actions from their perceived plan, and this is contrary to our roles, for we can help you make decisions, but it always has to be your choice. You have the free will to follow whatever path you choose, and we can only encourage you—in a very nice way—to follow your heart.
>
> It is interesting that when someone is described as being haunted, it has the worst connotations, with demons and poltergeists reigning terror. And yet when you see something that is beautiful beyond compare, it can be described as hauntingly beautiful. Strange how the same word can have such contrasting meanings. Just part of the way of life on Earth.

After some breathwork a few days later, Eileen had this to say:

> To be truly at one with yourself—your inner self, the real you—you must rein in the mind and its physical practicalities and bring into balance the thoughts that come from the heart, for it is from the heart that your true feelings, hopes and desires reside. It is often the case that the mind takes priority, and this can separate you from your true self, for it feeds on logic and human traits. You know that you are only partly developed in human form and that the greater part of you resides in spirit. Your soul and the human mind can sometimes have conflicts, and when this is the case, most often because you are present in a physical world, the mind takes precedence.
>
> To bring the soul and the human mind together and to be in unison with one another is to project your whole self, and your whole self is one of joy, compassion and empathy. These qualities can get lost when the physical aspects of the mind override the spiritual aspects of the soul.
>
> As souls we are androgynous with a blend of both masculine and feminine traits, but as we incarnate, we choose to be physically one or the other, although our inner self retains both. This is part of the contrasts we experience, but we should always play host to that gender that is not physically apparent, for to portray aspects of both is to give us balance.
>
> Be proud of the masculinity that is your physical being and cherish that which is feminine in you. This will give you balance and allow you to become whole.

As with so many messages I get, they can apply to everyone, for we all have our concerns and misgivings, even if we don't outwardly show them. There is a need for balance in all things in life, for the pendulum not to swing too far in either direction, but sadly this seems not to be the case with so many decisions that are made, not only by us as individuals but also as governments. Vision, foresightedness and balance are the keys to harmonious relationships around the world, not only between countries but also with the Earth itself. As Eileen has said, we have all come from the one Source. If we could truly see this and know that we are all part of the one spiritual family, if we hold no judgement over others, respect one another, and accept each individual for who they are, and if we aim for a higher spiritual awakening within us, then conflicts and violence will be a thing of the past. Eileen reiterates this after I asked her a question on what happens to animals when they pass into spirit.

> Animals and humans are all part of the same Source, for there is only one Source, and everything that is created, both in spirit and in physical is derived from that Source. But just as animals and humans, trees and flowers, have a different core energy that makes them what they are, there is a difference in the way the energy is formed in animals compared to that of humans.
>
> All in spirit have unconditional love for one another, but when reincarnated, especially on Earth, the human energy is such, with its amnesia blocking past events, that it is basically starting from scratch. As humans grow in their earthly physical bodies, they are influenced by the society they are brought up in, and invariably this does not include unconditional love; in fact, just the opposite is mostly the case.
>
> For animals, when they reincarnate on the Earth plane, they have no such amnesia, and so, especially with those species that are closest friends with humans—pets—they exude unconditional love. We as humans can learn a great deal from our pets in this area. When an animal dies, it does not need to be met by loved ones to help in the transition because it has the memory of spirit. Although there are no boundaries in the spirit world, animals and humans as

spirits do not usually merge. Even though we are all from the one Source energy, the form of that energy differs, and so the animals have different learning processes from humans and are therefore separated from us to a degree. That is not to say if you had a pet on Earth that was very special to you, you would not see it in spirit; both your needs are taken into account, and if beneficial to one or the other or both, a reunion will take place.

We are all one, from the tiniest molecule to the largest structure, all from the one and only Source. Every race, every creed, every colour, every living thing on that Earth of yours, every rock and stone—all one, all part of each other. As humans we should realise this life and Earth-changing fact, for if we understood the real meaning of this, then we would not have conflict, we would not destroy nature for our own narrow-minded opportunities, and the world would indeed be a utopia.

Ah! The promises of theoretical perfection. When it comes down to it, love—unconditional love—is the salvation of the world.

Her words are always so inspiring and meaningful to me. They bring me so much comfort and reinforce my knowing that she is with me to encourage me along this new path in my life, for I am doing things that I would never have even considered before. There has been a whole new world open up for me; my spirituality has soared, and the incredible people I have met and befriended have lifted my soul to new heights.

Although I still miss the physical Eileen that I knew, the spiritual one is still beside me and has guided me to new levels of understanding. Her profound wisdom is breathtaking, and I am so grateful for this awesome connection.

Chapter 6

Signs and Cryptic Messages

Since Eileen has made her transition, I have received many signs from her that she is with me. At first she brought the lorikeets to me, and they still buzz me at times with a cheerful chirp as they go past. I have found numerous feathers, especially when I have just asked her to give me a sign, sometimes in the strangest of places. On occasions I have heard a song that answers a thought I have had, and of course there is the tangible proof right in front of me every time I finish a writing session with her.

In numerology, I am told that if we see the number 444, it means that our angels are telling us they are around us and to look out for the signs they leave for us, for they are wanting us to make a stronger connection with not only them but also with our higher self, that part of us that resides in spirit and can bring light and graciousness to us and the planet as a whole.

This number can be seen in a wide variety of situations, the most common, perhaps, being the time on a digital clock.

In the weeks following Eileen's transition, both my oldest daughter and I saw this many times. It was not uncommon for one or the other of us to wake through the night at exactly that time, but there were many other occasions when this number showed up. One particular day, I had taken my car in for a service, my daughter was with me, and while it was getting serviced we went for a walk around town. The first encounter with this number was when a bus passed with the route number 444, then a parked car had a phone number on it that included 444 in it, and when we went back to pick up the car, there was a car in the showroom, all ready for delivery, with just 444 on its number plate. It seems our angels were really trying to get through to us that they, including Eileen, were right there with us.

But there have been some instances where she has really validated her presence. Cryptic messages that seem to mean nothing at the time but turn out to be significant are one way, and events that happen that would otherwise be hard to explain are another way. It is at these times that my heart is filled with joy in the absolute knowing my girl is still with me.

At the end of March 2019, I was continuing my conversations with Eileen when I had the first of what was to be a series of cryptic but important messages from Eileen. I was trying to connect with her to do more writings and didn't seem to be getting anything in answer to a question I had put when I got the message to tell Helena, who was in Bali at the time, to be cautious of the man in green. I didn't think much of it at the time, putting it down to just an odd thought, but it kept coming and was very persistent. It was late, so I tried to put it out of my mind and went to bed, still thinking it was just a figment of my imagination.

The following day I had my two friends over for some Reiki and mentioned it to them, as it was still in my mind. They said I should definitely message Helena, which I did that evening, and to my surprise and absolute joy, she replied that she had had the same message from Eileen. She then messaged me back to say that a man in a green shirt had tried to rip her off for $100 at the money exchange!

In the morning I had gone to see Irene to start a course called Warriors, Settlers and Nomads, which would help me understand the makeup of my personality. During the session we talked about how I sometimes still had doubts that I was connecting to Eileen when doing these writings and how Eileen keeps saying that I need to believe totally, for although when I read the writings I know it hasn't come from me, when I am writing I used to have the thought, "Is it just me thinking this, or is it really a connection to my beautiful Eileen, because surely I couldn't be able to do this?" But after what happened, I was completely convinced that I AM doing this. I DO have the most incredible connection with my beautiful soulmate, and together we can make a difference and bring comfort to those who think they have lost loved ones.

This was so awesome. I thanked Eileen for getting through to me this way to dispel any doubts we were in fact doing this together. She must have been thinking, "About time! What does it take to convince him?" but she said:

> Now that you truly believe and have the knowledge that we are indeed connected, you will find more opportunities to help those in need. Helena needed to be forewarned, and I knew if I gave you both the message it would resonate, but it still took the girls to convince you to send the message—stubborn! It is truly wonderful that you have come to the realisation we are connected. You now know that when I talk to you, it doesn't seem strange or different, just thoughts that come. In time you will recognise the difference between your thoughts and my messages. We are truly blessed with this connection; you are always in my thoughts as I am in yours. We are a great team, and don't forget it!

A couple of days later, she let me know she was around me in a very different way. I had just arrived home from work and turned on my laptop to find it was in aeroplane mode, something I never use.

I jokingly asked Eileen if she had done it and if she was getting tech savvy now, because in life she had only a very basic knowledge of computers, just enough to do what she wanted. All I got as an answer was *"wait and see"*.

In the middle of that night I woke and heard a sound like a pneumatic drill, which seemed to be coming from the other side of the house. I went into the lounge room, and it was the speakers of the audio system making the noise, so I thought I had better turn it off at the wall. Then I saw my house phone lighting up, then turning off, then lighting up again—I'd never seen that before! I also turned it off at the wall but then noticed the DVD player was on, so I turned it off with the remote, only to find it turn on again. I did this a couple of times with the same result, so I turned it off at the wall as well. I thought I should probably turn the printer off, as it was in sleep mode and the light was blinking, so I pressed the power button, which immediately turned it off only to turn on and then off two more times. I also turned that off at the wall! I tried to turn a couple of lights on, but there was no power, yet when I went back to bed the phone handset in the bedroom still had a red light glowing, but the digital clock was off. They were both plugged into the same power point.

When I got up in the morning, there was power, and all seemed okay, so I put some washing on and went for my half-hour morning walk. When I got back, I hung the clothes out and came in to check something on my laptop; the power was off, so I checked with my neighbour, who confirmed the power was still off. Now I am not a great believer in coincidence anymore, so maybe I didn't have to wait too long to "wait and see"!

On another occasion, I was thinking about what ways those in spirit can give us signs that they are around us and was going out to hang out the washing. There at the bottom of the steps was a small but colourful lorikeet feather. Later that day when I was in my bedroom, I felt something under my foot; it was a bobby pin. I had vacuumed the floor just the previous day and know it wasn't there before. There was not even a container with bobby pins in the room. Just Eileen letting me know that she is with me in yet another way.

A few days later I went and saw my friend and counsellor, Irene. She asked me what I had been up to since seeing her last, and I was talking about how Helena had suggested I ask Eileen about the signs spirits use to let us know they are around us. While we were talking, there was a noise that came from the lounge room adjacent to where we were. Irene went to see what it was but couldn't find anything, so we continued our conversation and thought no more about it.

When I got home, Irene had emailed me with a photo of a candle that had fallen over; it was a thick candle that was in a candlestick holder. She had previously told me her dad lets her know he is around by knocking something over! How good was that, giving us a sign when we were just talking about them? So I think there were four of us there that day: Eileen and me, and Irene and her dad.

I do enjoy going for walks in nature, and for the most part it is a rewarding experience, but on some days during the warmer periods, it is hard to be able to walk alone, especially in the bush, as there are those who like to tag along to taunt you. Let me introduce you to the Australian bush fly. They are only small, but what they lack in size is more than made up for by their numbers and determination. Determination—that is, to bore into every available orifice they can find; your ears, eyes, nose and mouth are all welcome targets, and if they are not avoiding what is known as the Aussie wave as you try to chase them away by flailing your arms about like a madman, legions of them take a ride on your back, and I'm sure if there were enough of them, they would carry you away.

On one such day I was walking along the coastal headland track between Gerringong and Kiama, and the flies were at their most determined, and their unrelenting attacks were making life miserable. It seemed there were thousands of them, and I was constantly chasing them. I was well into my walk when they arrived and had a good half hour to reach the sanctuary of my car. I said to Eileen, "Can't you get rid of these flies, at least for a while?" Less than a minute later, the wind came up strongly, the flies were gone, and I had relief. Now that's what I call divine intervention.

She has helped me out this way a number of times; I was going to bed one night and could hear a dog barking, not too close, but loud enough to be annoying. I was talking to Eileen with her picture in my hand as I always do, and the dog was very persistent. You know that sound—"yap yap yap", pause, "yap yap yap". It seemed to be going on forever, so I asked Eileen if she could make it stop, and instantly there was quiet. This happened on a few occasions.

My second cryptic message came in July 2019. I had sat down to talk to Eileen when I heard the message, *"Ask Helena about her time in Florence"*. Helena had been to Europe with her husband, who had some business dealings there. I knew they had travelled to France and Italy but didn't know exactly where, and I hadn't spoken to her since she returned. When I caught up with her a few weeks later, I asked her about the trip, and she said that of all the places they visited, Florence was where she had the best experiences, especially the spiritual ones. She had a special connection to the place, as she had lived there in past lives and was able to tap into significant aspects of those times.

In October 2019 I had my third cryptic message; once again it was when I was hoping for an answer to a question but was getting nothing, then the thought came into my mind, *"The garden gnome has stories to tell, so please don't throw him down the well."* A week or so later, I found out that there was a lady who loved gnomes and had her garden filled with them; her husband had just transitioned to spirit and was contacting her.

Another strange message was *"The yellow dog is in the ashtray"*. I really had no idea what that could mean, but once again after a few weeks the message had meaning. A lady's dog, which was a golden retriever, had recently passed away, and she was having trouble deciding what to do, whether to have it buried or cremated. Her belief was that if the dog was cremated, it would not return to spirit, but she wasn't sure about burial either. She eventually decided to have it cremated, hence the dog in the ashtray!

Then there was the message *"The chocolate lady has gone"*. This was a reference to a family who made chocolates; the mother had recently transitioned. They were people I didn't know, and I only found out through Helena.

These messages seemed to be the oddest of thoughts when they first popped into my head, and to start with, I was ready to dismiss them as nonsense, but no matter how strange they may have seemed at the time, all have been validated at a later date and are another way Eileen confirms to me she is around me.

In June 2020, on the day of our 50th wedding anniversary, I was at the clothesline ready to hang out some sheets when I heard a soft chirp. I turned around to see a lorikeet on one of the bars of the clothesline, not a metre away. I said hello, and it chirped back, so I kept talking to it, and it chirped as though it was answering me. I continued to hang out the sheets, which meant rotating the line. The bird stayed where it was, and we kept "chatting", and it stayed there until I had finished. As I finished, it turned its back on me, and when I walked towards the house, it flew away. I have no doubt that this was Eileen's way of wishing us a happy anniversary.

Two days before, late at night when I had finished all that I was doing and was at a bit of a loose end, I was sitting in front of the TV, which was turned off. The TV has a Samsung badge just below the screen, which lights up when it is on and goes out when the TV is off. I was telling Eileen how much I missed her not being physically with me when the badge lit up even though the TV didn't turn on. Yet another instance of her letting me know she is with me.

On another occasion, I was out for a walk and spotted a feather on the path; it was a pure white feather from a cockatoo. A little later I came across a magpie feather, and I said to Eileen that these were all very well but common around these parts; how about something different like a peacock feather? No, I didn't come across any peacock feathers on the rest of the walk; in fact, I didn't come across any more feathers at all, so when I got home I said maybe that was too hard. Two nights later I was watching a program on the TV about antiques where experts explain about items people have brought along to value. One item was a Hawaiian ceremonial dress made from feathers, and the main feature was outlined in peacock feathers. So I figure Eileen did bring them to me after all!

I watched a series called "Surviving Death", a programme that delves into the lives of those who have recently lost a loved one and takes the viewer along their journeys, their encounters with mediums, and their reactions to the information received and also the signs they see.

There were two sisters whose 97-year-old mother was ready to pass. They asked her to send them a cardinal bird to let them know she had arrived in heaven safely. A short while after the mother had passed, a cardinal landed on one of their shoulders; they were able to hold it, and when they let it go, it came back to them, then flew into a tree and left. Such a positive sign their mother was contacting them. I thought at the time how awesome that was, what a great and obvious sign, and I said as much to Eileen. A day later, I was in my garden putting out food for the ever-present lorikeets when one landed on my shoulder, and I was able to hand-feed it, something that had never happened before or since.

This is just a sampling of the signs and messages I get, but the important thing to know is that we should always be aware that those in spirit are around us, and we should be recognising the signs when they present. It is far too easy to be swept up in the physicality of life and miss these moments of validation. Some may be sceptical and try to renounce them as figments of our imagination, but there is the key, for our imagination is our inspiration and our connection to spirit as it comes from within, just as our intuition is our inner wisdom, hence the word in-tuition: learning from within and from our higher self.

There is an important lesson in all this, for if we want to connect with spirit, we have to have an open mind and be prepared for any possibilities. With my first cryptic message experience—the "green man" incident—I was ready to fob it off as just a random thought, even though I was very aware that Eileen was sending me signs and we were connecting through our writings. It is so easy to miss the signs when we get swept up in our daily lives, but in saying that, we still need to be grounded as we are here in this incarnation to focus on the density that is our life on Earth, so there will always be signs that we miss. But when they do show up, even if it is a strange thought, ask yourself, could this be my loved one's way of connecting with me? In most cases the answer will be yes, and if you truly believe this, you can take a great deal of comfort from the knowledge that your loved ones are indeed with you and trying to communicate with you. You haven't lost them, only the physical aspect of them.

You may know the story of the man who was on the roof of his house with floodwaters rising. He had great faith in God and was sure God would save him. As the waters rose, two men in a rowboat came by to help him off the roof, but he refused their help, saying that God would save him. A little while later, when the water was lapping at his feet, a helicopter came to lift him off the roof, but again he refused, saying God will save him. Eventually the waters rose and he drowned. When he arrived at the pearly gates, he was met by God. He was so surprised that he had drowned and that God had not saved him, and he told God as much, to which God replied, "Well, who do you think sent the boat and the helicopter!"

The man had completely missed the signs that God was helping him, being blinded by the limitations he had set on how God would help. He didn't recognise the boat or helicopter as God's help, perhaps expecting some other kind of special miracle.

This can be the same for us if we limit how we expect signs from our loved ones to come to us. Take the peacock feather sign; I could have simply missed what Eileen showed me if I had expected to see an actual peacock feather while walking.

> From the moment we leave our earthly bodies, our main priority is to let those left behind who are close to us know that we are all right, that the trauma, pain and suffering that often accompany us leading to our transition are over, and that we are returning to our true home in spirit. In my case, while I was in a coma, I would slip in and out of my physical body, and when I decided it was time to go home, that Michael was ready for my transition and had given me his blessing, I left my first sign for him in the words of that song, which I knew would tell him exactly what was to happen: that although I was no longer physically with him, I would always be with him in spirit, no matter where he goes. This was important, for it would give him the incentive to keep looking for my signs.
>
> For the most part, humans are not very good at believing in what they cannot see, feel or touch, so we keep sending signs in all kinds of forms to try to convince them we are around. Sometimes it is something simple like a feather or a butterfly with its striking colours. Other times we will use birds or animals in unusual situations to try to catch your attention, for they are happy for us to interact with them in this way. We may come to you in your dreams, and yet other times we will be more forceful, such as at the time of the power cut. Michael and I have been fortunate, for he always believed I would contact him and was actively looking for any signs. During our life on Earth we were very close, and he knew of times when my mother had contacted me after her transition, so he knew of the possibilities.
>
> It is often hard at first for those left behind to get through the overwhelming grief that can really block our attempts to connect,

but we are persistent, and if they are willing and open to all possibilities, then it will happen. But remember that just as every person is unique, so too is the relationship they will have with those in spirit. What may happen for one may not for another, and this is why it is so important that you do not compare your connection with those of others, for your connection is the ideal one for your present level of acceptance.

One of the biggest resistances to human connection with spirit is the person's religious upbringing, because so many religions tell the fable of an afterlife containing heaven and hell that is completely separate from our life on Earth, so the fear is that their loved ones may have gone in the wrong direction, so to speak, and even if they haven't, they certainly would not be able to make a connection. This is truly fiction, for there is no hell, except maybe hell on Earth; there is no damnation, and there is no judgement presided over by a vengeful God. Our Creator has only unconditional love for all of us and has given us free will to use our earthly incarnations to experience that which we cannot whilst in spirit.

The cryptic messages, as Michael calls them, are another way we can try to convince you that we are around you. Although the message may at first seem strange, there is always a truth in it, and it is for you to find out what that truth is. When you do you will know it is from us, for its true meaning will be revealed, often as an event in someone else's life. Some messages may be missed as you are preoccupied in the business of living your life, and this is how it should be, for your main purpose is to learn from your physical experiences and not to be so involved with the spiritual aspects of yourselves that the lessons of the current incarnation are lost.

If you absolutely know, believe and trust that we are with you, then you will always be open to our signs. We send you many, so even if you miss some, you will pick up on others. To know, believe and trust are the keys to a strong and continuous connection, and love is the binding factor.

From that first morning when I woke to the words of the song that told me Eileen would always be with me, every time I get a sign from her, it gives me a feeling of such joy and is a reminder of those words. It confirms to me that I am not alone, that my girl is still with me and will be forever.

Others I have spoken to say the signs they receive give them comfort in the knowledge their loved ones have not gone forever but are with them whenever they need them, and it also takes the fear of death away—for, as Eileen keeps telling me, there really is no death, only a transition from physical to spiritual. It is a transference from one dimension to another and a raising of our vibration from the density that is the human reality to the light of spirit.

Although I have said that we need to know, believe and trust in order to make a strong connection, at times those in spirit will come to those who don't believe.

Ruth's husband is a person who did not really believe in spirituality and was very much firmly grounded in the physical world.

They have a few horses, and recently his favourite one called Smokey died; he was at its side when it passed. The horse was buried, and that night he told Ruth he was sitting at its grave, when he thought he saw Smokey nearby, but said it couldn't have been. Two days later, he heard Smokey whinny, and later on that day, a bird with a red breast—not one they normally have around the property—came and landed on the seat beside him, looking at him and chirping. It was so unusual he asked if it was Smokey. It then flew over to a table near a door where Smokey used to stand and again looked back at him, chirping. This convinced him that the bird was definitely brought to him by the spirit of the horse.

The following day, Ruth was walking on her property when she heard a bird chirping; she said it sounded like the words "look up". When she looked towards where the sound was coming from, there was the same bird looking down at her. The next minute it was gone, but she didn't see or hear it fly away. This may be the turning point in

Ruth's husband's outlook and perhaps the start of his connection to those in spirit around him.

It often takes a significant event in our lives for us to start seeing the universal truths about the cycles of the lives we travel. For me, it took a long time to get interested in spirituality even though Eileen was, but her return home was the real catalyst that propelled me towards the beliefs I now hold and the truths that I have discovered.

It is not just our loved ones who are looking out for us; our guides and angels are always with us too. We may be physically alone in a room, but that room is literally busting at the seams with those in spirit who are around us. Isn't that just the most comforting feeling to know that we are indeed immortal with a family of caring souls that we are a part of?

Chapter 7

More Wisdom From Spirit

The information I receive from Eileen is always full of wisdom and, in many cases, very profound. She often brings me viewpoints that I would never have thought of—something she used to do when she was here, but now she is in spirit and has a much wider perspective, her insights are completely on another level. To have this amazing connection with the love of my life makes me feel so blessed, so fortunate to hear her words and to be able to understand that there is so much more to our being than just this physical body we are in, and to know that we are indeed immortal as souls and that this journey we call life is just one of many episodes on our path to divinity.

Please understand that I do not have special powers; often when I attend spiritual meetings where we do meditations, I am the one who can't hold my focus. You may know the scenario; I am preparing to meditate, concentrating on my breathing, just getting into the rhythm of it when I start to think, "Maybe my car's tyre pressures need topping up" or similar thoughts, hardly conducive to good meditation! And I am the one who is in awe of those who have truly mastered this art.

In most cases I am the student surrounded by masters, and yet I have this wonderful connection with Eileen and am able to bring her words to paper. Even this does not happen every time; I may try to connect for weeks without success, and usually this is because I am not in the right frame of mind. The physicality of life gets in the way, and the mind sets its own priorities, much to my chagrin at times. But when we connect and the words flow, it is the most amazing feeling to know that the words I write are from across the dimensions. I still wonder at times if it is my thoughts that I am writing, but my doubts are allayed when I read back what is written. There have even been occasions when I have had to ask Helena if she can explain what a particular piece of text means.

These messages that bring many of the truths of the universes to us—that give us an insight into the reality of our being—are very special, for they can dispel the fear of death and bring us the knowledge that will bring us comfort and peace in times of grief. And for this reason I would like to share with you more of the wisdom from spirit that Eileen has channelled through me, for although these messages are in answer to my questions, many of them may resonate with you.

M: Do we have guardian angels?

E: *While we are incarnated on Earth, we all have those who watch over us. Often they are as I am to you—loved ones who have since passed—and mostly they are from your soul group. But at times, when the need arises, those who are our guiding angels whilst we are home may come to us. These can be the Ascending Masters—Jesus, the Archangel Michael and others, who will come to us when called upon by our peers in spirit, generally in times where even greater support than we can give is needed.*

For the most part, your guiding angels are your guides that help you in spirit; they are not there to protect you but to give you options and to encourage you. You always have a lot of entities around you, and they may change as circumstances change, but I am always with you—that is our bond. Those imaginary friends you had when you were young were not as imaginary as you might think. You can even be visited by your soul in spirit at times when you require your whole self to progress. Be sure in the knowledge that you are never alone.

M: Are mediums more advanced souls?

E: *Those that you call mediums are tuning into the spiritual energies that are around all of you. Everyone has the ability to do this, but most of you are not in the right vibration to connect this way. The souls of mediums and clairvoyants are not necessarily more advanced; it is all a matter of the ability to tune in. There are very advanced souls incarnating on Earth who would not seem to be spiritual at all, and some mediums are souls who are quite young.*

As the news from around the world is brought to you by various mediums such as newspapers, the radio and television, so the news from spirit is brought to you by those you call mediums, and just as the world news can get distorted in its delivery to you, so too can the medium distort the message from spirit. A good medium will simply allow the energies to flow and be translated in as accurate a way as possible.

Everyone has the ability to receive messages from spirit if they tune in and listen to their intuition, for their intuition speaks to them from that part of themselves that remains in spirit.

M: Do spells work and is there magic?

E: *Spells are just another tool you can use for attraction and manifestation. If you believe that casting a spell and the ritual involved will attract something, or someone, or a situation into your life, then it will be, for it is the power of thought that makes spells appear to work. Remember when you buried an apple to get rid of a wart? When that happened, it was your thought process rather than the actual burying of the apple that caused the wart to disappear. In saying this, spells should never be used on another because they could only work if the other person knows of the spell and attaches thought to it. We all have our own journeys on Earth, and to mystically tamper with another is not part of it.*

Magic is all around you: the magic of new life and the magic of what we are doing now with our awesome connection. Magic is in the eye of the beholder; to see the magic of nature in the growth and blooming of a flower is to be part of that magic. Magicians' magic is all a clever illusion, which can seem real when you can't see the process, but life is magical always. Seek the magic in your life, and magical things will happen.

It has been over five years since Eileen returned to spirit, but I still haven't been able to get rid of her clothes. I know there is really no point in keeping them, but it's hard to let go. So I asked Eileen how I can get into the right mindset to bring myself to dispose of them.

E: Earthly chattels are of no use to me now, this you know, this you understand, but the questions are:
1. *What do they mean to you? Are you holding onto them as they are tangible evidence of my past presence?*
2. *Are you holding onto them because you feel if you let them go, in some way you will be letting go of me?*
3. *Are you holding onto them because you can't bear to part with them?*

These are the questions you need to ask yourself, for if the answer to any one of them is yes, then you are not ready to part with them, no matter how illogical that may seem. They are clothes for the physical being that I am no longer, but know this—whether you part with them or not, this will have absolutely no effect on the bond we have, for they are just things, and what we have goes far beyond the need for physical things.

As they are now, lying in drawers, they are of no benefit, for even though you may think they are significant in that they are what was once part of my life, it is of no importance now; I am spirit, and they are physical. Physical objects should be utilised by physical beings. If you donate them to a charity, other physical beings will benefit from them far more than you do.

You know our connection is strong, and any thought that removing the clothes from the house would weaken it is illthought. But you must be ready in yourself to take the step, which will be another progression in your new life, moving on to the next episode and moving forward. Casting them off will help release the past and propel you towards your future— another hindrance let go.

I am with you always, always as close as you will let me be—clothes or not!

M: Have I achieved goals in my life that have been beneficial for my soul's growth? Do we need to live challenging lives for our soul to grow?

E: *A soul's growth does not necessarily require hardship and challenging situations. You have learnt in this incarnation what it is to truly love someone from a human perspective, and this is a big step to have taken considering your past lives. It is what we learn in our lives that is important for soul growth and advancement, whether it be from hardships and traumas or from recognising the blessings we have in each life. Regardless of the emotions attached, it is the choices we make that denote the advancement of our soul. You could go through a life with what seems like not a care in the world, but it is how you react to bliss or banishment that allows your soul to grow.*

Look back at this life and see just what you have achieved. You have taken some very large steps up the ascendancy; think about your life and see the progress you have made. Try looking at it as though you are watching a movie, and see what you find.

M: Your coming into my life was the best thing that could have happened to me, and I hope I was as good as I could be to you. I always supported you in your projects and loved to see you excel in everything you did, but it was you being in my life that made it worthwhile, and I feel that my contributions to our family were much less than yours. Even now when you are no longer in the physical, you are my guiding light, and this love I have for you goes deep into my being.

You were the carer, you were the healer, and you were the one to reach out to others. I was there beside you and happy to follow. Sure, I went to work and provided financial stability for us, but that was only with your support and our being in sync with each other when it came to money matters and all the philosophies of life. The only way I can see my soul advance would be through being in that wonderful relationship with you for the best part of my life.

E: *You have done so much more than you give yourself credit for, you must try not to look through the glasses of negativity and instead see all the positive things you have done. I will give you some clues, but it is you who should be seeing them. Our life together was very successful, for we both worked for harmony, and although you say you supported me, you were my strength to do those things you talk about. Your support for me in every situation was instrumental in our success, and in those times when I was going through extreme stress, you were my rock—many others would not have supported and encouraged me as you did. And in those last two years of my incarnation, you were there for me always, even though my fear was that when you went to work, you would not return. You did all you could to help me, taking me to so many practitioners to try to find answers. For that I am eternally grateful.*

So think about your life from a positive aspect, and you will find that although you did not reshape the world, you have done some amazing things for those who are close to you.

And there is more to come; you will have a significant impact on many if you follow the path you are now on, and your soul will evolve to greater levels because of the life you have led.

M: How much influence do our human DNA and ancestral links and the personality of the soul have on our human personality?

E: *Ancestral links and our environment when growing up may contribute to our life's preferences, but they are not part of the makeup of our personality. Everyone's personality is unique, just as their DNA is, but this does not necessarily mean the DNA produces the personality; it is certainly one aspect that can contribute to the whole, but it is not the leading factor. Our personality is made up from a wide variety of sources, and DNA is just one of them. If DNA were the sole contributor to personality, we would find that those born to the same mother and father would have similar personalities, but that is not the case.*

A combination of factors, which include DNA, but also the preference of the human brain, and input from the soul, all contribute to our personality, and the events of past lives are only partially relevant, as the amnesia that keeps those details from us reduces their influence. You know from your course with Irene that personality has several facets, and each one of these can come to the fore at different times, but there will always be one dominant aspect, and this is often a blending of the human mind and that of the soul.

M: Do our past lives have an influence on events in the present life? Is there such a thing as karma?

E: *From the moment we are created from source energy our souls are searching for the truths of the universes. We create human lives to experience that which will bring us closer to the answers we are seeking at that point in our development. As we evolve, more questions arise, so more incarnations are created to find the answers, and as we progress through each incarnation we are growing, and even though we are blocked with amnesia, our higher self is putting all the pieces of our experiences over all lifetimes together. Each life is like part of a jigsaw puzzle, and as each life is completed, the picture of the whole begins to appear.*

Past lives don't necessarily influence the present, but they are all interconnected. When you talk of karma, you may be thinking along the lines of an eye-for-an-eye type of process, but this is not the case. Karma, or at least what you call karma, is purely conjectural; it does not mean that if you carry out a wrongdoing (which is only wrong in your eyes, for there is no right or wrong, there just is), you will have that same action perpetrated on you at a later date.

The word karma is misused. When we examine our lives once we have returned home, we may see a part of our lives where we carried out certain actions or were in a particular state of health, and we might decide that on our return to the playhouse of life, we will experience the opposite. This is not karma; this is the CHOICE we make independently when in spirit before incarnating. Your question relates to present circumstances, and you have this thought of payback for past deeds. This is not so; all incarnating experiences are for the soul's growth. Some of us make it harder than others, but we are all aiming for the same eventual result, which is to be able to evolve to the point when we can reunify with Source.

Past lives will present themselves when it is provident for them to do so; think not of past lives or karma, for these are all from times afar. It is NOW that you are living, and so now is where your thoughts should be, for now is as real as real can be. Live in the now and enjoy the moment. Too many lives have been squandered by focusing on past events or what may happen in the future. Right now you have your lovely daughter winging her way across the skies to be with you—what an exciting time for both of you. Be in the now, and enjoy every minute together, for as you know, life is short, and making the most of every moment should be everyone's goal.

Cherish the times together just as we cherished our times, even if we didn't show it at times. Our life was truly one made in heaven—well, in spirit anyway. Love is always with us, remember we are bonded with the unbreakable power of love, compassion, empathy and courage.

I sometimes draw tarot cards to get a reading, and at one time in July of 2019, I drew three cards. The first card for the past was The Hermit, the second for the present was The Hanged Man Reversed, and for the future, I drew The Emperor. Eileen had used tarot before, so rather than follow the text in the book that accompanied the cards, I thought I would ask her about them.

E: Tarot is an ancient art of divination that allows you to access your inner self. It dates back at least to Egyptian times when pharaohs ruled the Earth, although it was not in the form of today's images. The Egyptian rulers used their form of tarot to seek wisdom of past mistakes and future scenarios to make decisions for the present. Though the format of the symbols and hieroglyphs has changed, the wisdom is still held in the modern-day cards. It was once believed that only those specially empowered could use and interpret tarot, but this never has been the case; everyone with an open mind and heart can use tarot.

You have drawn these cards to give you an insight into what your intuition, your inner self and your higher self are wanting to display to you. There is nothing mystical about which cards you pick and their meanings; the cards will always be the right ones for you at the time they are drawn. When you read the detail of each card for past, present and future information, you will always find a truth in them.

Your cards are showing you that, not just in the past of this life, but of other past lives, you have been a loner in many ways, maybe not the hermit that is depicted, but often shunning others. But you have had a wisdom about you that you have only shared with a select few. The card that depicts your present is the reversed hanged man, which is showing you that this is a time of great change in your life—change that will grow your soul and will bring out the wisdom from within. It is a time when you will bring joy to many with your words and deeds. And the Emperor—the future—tells you there is a great wealth coming to you, not necessarily in the monetary aspect, but a wealth of precious gifts that you will bestow on others with the wisdom you are gaining from your present situation. I have said before that you have a great deal of work to do before you complete this incarnation, and by seeing these events through *and bringing the wisdom to the world, you will have made a great contribution to mankind.*

I am so excited for you, for although you may go through some mental hardships on the journey, they will pass soon and you will focus on those elements that are important to us all, both here in spirit and on Earth. Have faith in yourself, for you have abilities you do not realise you have.

Just as your daughter knows and BELIEVES that her loved ones in spirit are with her, so too should you BELIEVE that I am always here, along with all your support team in spirit, to help and encourage you in all your endeavours. Do everything that feels right from your heart, and you will bring joy to many.

Blessed be, I love you as you do me.

M: It is said that since 2012, the energies on Earth have changed. What is actually happening with these new energies?

E: *In spirit there is no linear time; the past is the present is the future. All things happen simultaneously, and what is happening is the realignment of the Earth's energy to the new remodelled spiritual energy that has been evolving since your year 2012. All things, both in spirit and in physical form, are energy; thoughts are energy, rocks are energy, people are energy, and all physical forms create their being with energy resonating at different frequencies. Those frequencies give rise to the form the energy takes: its density, shape, size, colour, etc.*

As we all vibrate at different frequencies, hence the unlimited shapes and styles we present. We are all attracted to different frequencies, this is why some will like a particular food whilst others will not. It is all about the contrasts we need to experience whilst in physical. Likewise, as all things spiritual and physical are derived from energy oscillating at different frequencies, so too are the different dimensions. If you were to tune in to the frequency of another dimension, then you would pass into it.

With the interaction between the Earth's present energy frequency as a whole and the new spiritual energy, there are times when the combination of frequencies will be such that dimensions will cross paths. At this time, physical entities can cross the dimensions momentarily, creating the illusion of something impossible to the eye of the beholder.

Know that this life is all part of the ongoing evolvement of the energies, both from spirit and from physical, for they are from the same original source.

M: Our consciousness level in spirit is much higher than in physical. Why don't we bring our spiritual consciousness level with us when we reincarnate?

E: *When we come into a new incarnation, there are many things that can affect our outcome in the human body. The human brain is powerful enough to resist our spiritual tendencies, and this is for a good reason: if we came into physical, whether it be on Earth or another similar planet, and we were totally as we are in spirit, then the whole process of reincarnation would be pointless. As I have said many times before, and those who speak the words of spiritual entities have also said, we reincarnate to experience the contrasts, the joys and the sadness, the light and the dark, and the "good" and the "bad", and if we were of the same level of consciousness as we are in spirit, there would be no learning from the contrasts. Our physical incarnations are necessary for our souls to experience the contrasts and to grow from those experiences.*

As our souls develop, we will bring more of our consciousness with us, but not all souls are at the same level of development, and the Earth's population's overall level depends on the advancement or otherwise of all souls on Earth. Until all souls reach a certain point of enlightenment, there will always be a difference in consciousness between the spirit world and the Earth, but we are all moving in the direction that causes our souls to evolve, albeit at different speeds. As each generation passes, the Earth's total level of consciousness rises, and only when it reaches that level where war and weapons are seen as unnecessary will this come to pass.

Take heart in the fact that any period of Earth's time, when compared to an earlier one, is an improvement, although in more recent times, especially since the energy shift at the time when prophecies said the world would end. The Earth is dawning a new age, and as more and more people are feeling the shift in energies, their levels of consciousness are rising. The more people who become in touch with the TRUTH and totally BELIEVE in it, the higher Earth's consciousness becomes. It is for those who, to put it in biblical terms, have "seen the light" to become the warriors of the new raised consciousness and to encourage all they come in contact with to see it too. There are many who are watching with pride to see the Earth move towards this goal.

M: If there is no linear time in spirit and you are around me on Earth with linear time, how does that work?

E: *This may be hard for you to understand, for it is your perception that comes from the dense matter that is the Earth and its contents. You have a perception of what your reality is based on your experiences and those that are around you, but what is reality? Reality is only what you perceive from your viewpoint from the density that is the Earth, but reality can be very different from the frequencies we resonate at in spirit, so it is all in the belief system you have been taught.*

What really is a mile or a kilometre? They are only measured distances which have been formulated by the human race. There is no such thing as a mile or kilometre; they are just measurements based originally on the average length of a human's foot. Time is another human invention, for it is with time that you can understand speed, as without time, there would be no concept of speed, and yet time is only relative to the frequency you are emitting. You have heard that the faster you travel, the shorter time becomes, so that if you could travel at the speed of light—and you can—then time would have the appearance of standing still. So it is with our frequencies.

Jasmine often talks about how those in spirit are travelling at the speed of light, while those on Earth move at a snail's pace. This is simplifying the process but is an easy way to understand. Basically, the higher the frequency you vibrate at, the less time has an effect on you. For us to be around you on Earth, we need to lower our frequency such that we can accommodate your earthly time spans. But we are also in spirit when we are with you, so we divide and conquer, so to speak, with differing vibrational frequencies for the two different energy levels.

If this does not make a lot of sense to you, just know that I am in spirit vibrating at spiritual levels, but I am also with you, tasting your world through you at your pace. As spiritual beings, we use our duality to be able to accomplish this.

Always with you, always in spirit, just as you are too. The difference is that as an incarnate of Earth with physical priorities, you don't connect to your higher self—that part of you who is in spirit—unless you go within and leave physicality behind, as in meditation.

M: I love you so much and miss you being physically with me. I would willingly join you now, but I know I need to complete my life's course, which includes the Camino walk and writing our book.

E: *Now let's have a look at us, at the beautiful connection and bond we have; you should rejoice each and every day for this perfect and special connection we have between us, for we are so special that we have this. Not everyone in every life attains this level of bonding across the dimensions, and we haven't in past incarnations. So it is a joyful thing that we have, to be so close, although you sometimes think so far.*

We are truly blessed during this time, and though you may think that if we were both in spirit we would be closer, the truth is we are as close as we can ever be, regardless of the fact that you are there on Earth and I am here at home in spirit. Just because the dimensions appear to separate us, our bond is eternal and can never be broken. For although I am in the spirit realm, I am also with you, beside you even though you may not see me or feel me; that will change in time—Earth time, that is. Be joyful, and we will be joyful together; rejoice in the immaculate perfection that is us. You need to lift yourself from the seriousness of life and see the joy and fun that is there. Look on the bright side; see the positives and relegate the negatives, for every situation has both. These are the contrasts that are what living on Earth is all about.

I love you dearly, you know this, and I want you to be happy. This is not just for your sake, for if you are happy, then our bond and connection can only become stronger. Be the warrior of happiness; search out the good in all and everything, for everything has good in it.

Lift your spirit, and as you do this, literally, you will lift your vibration level; the more you can do this, the more you will, as you say, feel me, hear me and see me. We are together, BELIEVE and TRUST and KNOW, just as you know there is no death, only a transition from one dimension to another, for we are all pure energy at the core, and energy CANNOT be destroyed. We are eternal beings, and that means we are going to BE forever, and as that is the case, why would we not want to savour and enjoy every moment of it?

Together we will complete the current incarnation of yours, we will complete the Camino, and we will complete the book. And then—well, let's just wait and see what amazing possibilities await us. It is with you that I am always, and with me you are always. Love cannot be conquered, and we have love. Oh! Do we have love!

M: Why is it that the death of a human usually involves sickness and deterioration? Why can't we just transition nicely?

E: There are many cases where humans do transition to spirit nicely, as you put it. The soul knows that it has completed the acts of play that were laid down for it to follow in its current life, and often, as the human they are attached to is old by modern human standards, they are ready to return home. The problem is, for a human to pass into spirit, they must first present a reason for doing so that is acceptable to the society they have lived in, and in most cases that requires the body to become unhealthy, for it would not be acceptable for a healthy person to just lie down and die, in a manner of speaking. So the body becomes sick in one way or another, which allows those who are close to acclimatise to the idea that their loved one is going to transition. The only time a healthy human will decide to return to spirit is when they arrange for what you would call an accident or violent situation to take place for them to transition.

Sickness and sadness that are attached to the transition are part of what is expected by society, anything else, apart from "accidents", would be completely impossible for most humans to comprehend. The process of grief after a loved one *has transitioned is very often the catalyst for a greater spiritual awareness for those left behind. Your own story attests to that. For a human to increase its spirituality is essential if their soul is to continue to grow towards its goal of divinity.*

There is no death; it only appears that way to those in physical who have not accessed their spirituality, and this can be through their religious beliefs that absolutely have no foundation in spirituality.

We all, as humans and souls, grow from the so-called death of a loved one, but as you very well know, this transition only makes those who have departed much closer than they could ever be while in physical. Blessed are the cycles we go through to enhance our soul growth; we are all immortal, and those who are our closest souls will be together with us for eternity, testing and learning together in our search for the knowledge of the universes.

M: Why is it we focus on the circumstances of a person's death rather than their achievements in life? Can you give us ideas on how to change this?

E: *Because we, as humans in general, do not understand or know the processes we go through for our soul's growth, the processes that are the cycles of life, death and reincarnation, and all that is within those processes, we see death as a time of sadness and darkness instead of a release and a triumphant return home to be whole once again as a complete soul.*

It is instilled in our consciousness by the Earthly society that we live in to be focusing on the dark side of life; just look at the content of the news services, there is mainly darkness with very little light, and this is carried over into most parts of our lives, which is why the human mind will focus on that which is considered bad rather than that which is good.

The contrasts we come to Earth to experience have both what you would call goodness and badness, although from a purely spiritual point of view, there is no good or bad; there just is. What we must do as humans is break that tradition of looking on the dark side and bring joy and light into our lives, for if we can do this, we will see the positives in all situations. We will know that the transition to spirit is just a part of the constant cycles that make us who we are, both spiritually and physically, over the aeons.

The logic says we should celebrate that part of a person's incarnation when they were living and learning—always the greater part of their life, for the period of transition is normally only a very short time when compared to the length of the incarnation as a whole. It is just like when we have a day with a hundred positives and one negative, why do we focus on the one negative when it has been far outweighed by the positives?

Look to the joy in life, know that everyone has written their basic story before incarnating, and know there are no accidents in the Universe. If you understand this—really understand this—then you will truly see the joy in every situation, for everyone involved is fulfilling their journey. Let the light in, and the light will lighten you and your perceptions of what is, for happiness is the goal of every single person on this planet; it is just that many do not know this.

In spirit there is a perpetual feeling of joy and wonder about all things, and we can see the achievements of those on Earth are best made when in a state of happiness and joy.

Look to the light, and the light will look to you.

M: I know that we as humans sign up for our lives and the various events in them, but what about animals? There have been so many killed by the bushfires?

E: *The soul of an animal is different from that of a human even though it comes from the same Source. The roles are different, and the perspective is different, just as the soul of a flower, the soul of a tree, the soul of a fish and the soul of the Earth are. All these souls were born from the same universal Source, and each plays its part in the life that is present on Earth, including the Earth itself. Animals, plants, the oceans and the Earth are nature itself, whereas the soul that is the human can only try to live in harmony with nature; it is not nature as such.*

Because the animals, plants, and trees are nature, then nature's forces are embodied in them, and when what you call natural disasters occur—which are not disasters at all, just nature playing out its role in conjunction with the energies of both the Earth and the Universe—then the process does include the returning of animal souls to their home base in the spirit world. The animals, especially the ones humans consider cute, although to spirit, all forms of life could be considered cute, can help unite the world's humanity when they are seen to be hurt or killed by the forces of nature, which are in fact their own forces or energies, for they are nature itself.

As humans sign up for different events to occur in their lives, usually for the soul to experience what it cannot in spirit, then nature is sometimes called upon to create these events. Nature, that is, the combination of animals, plant life, the oceans and the Earth, all play their part in bringing about the event. This is all part of the black and the white that is life on Earth.

M: I notice at our meetings with Helena, there are a few in the group who, like me, are not keen on loud, noisy crowds.

E: *It is not unusual for those with strong spiritual connections to feel somewhat apart from the mainstream population, but this must be kept in balance, for to focus solely on spirit is to separate the mortal from their mortality, to separate themselves from the earthly reality that is life on Earth.*

The monks of old, and even some still to this day, shut themselves away in monasteries and completely shut out what is the real world in search of their ultimate connection to their chosen religion. Though this may seem very noble to those who look up to them, they are completely missing the point of life on Earth: to experience the contrasts, to experience life to the full, to experience love and joy, despair and loneliness, and all the differences we need to experience for soul growth.

Those who have a strong connection to spirit will, by that connection, have different aims and goals than those who are completely ensconced in the earthly ways of greed, money and possessions, and their idea of enjoyment is very different from the earthly predominance of drink and fast cars, so to speak. Spiritual enjoyment comes with much less reliance on the physical, but when those spiritually aware come together, the meeting of like-minded souls brings a great deal of comfort, knowledge and awareness. Earthly social gatherings are lacking in all these qualities and are often overwhelmed with loud music, drink and flirtations.

It is for all of you to find the social engagement that suits you best. For you, you have never liked being around drinkers and gamblers, and you have always felt uncomfortable in those situations, yet you can be with a roomful of spiritual souls, just like the gathering of a few Saturdays ago, and you can feel totally at ease, even if in awe of the others. The vibration of such a gathering is much higher than that of a social party, and you will always find souls who are vibrating at similar levels to you. The uncomfortable feeling you get at earthly socials is caused by an imbalance of the vibrations in the room, an inharmonious blend.

M: When I look back at my life, especially when we were together, we had a truly wonderful time together, raising our family and enjoying all our experiences. I would not change any of it, even the traumatic events that helped us grow. But if I look at the wisdom and achievements of people like Helena, and I see those in the group who, at such an early stage of their lives, are finding their purpose and connections to spirit, I ask myself, was I just drifting along, content to be with you and not truly seeking my life's purpose? I feel that now you are no longer a physical part of my life, that I am starting all over again, needing to grasp the wisdom and make a real difference to the world, but I am going to need another 70 years!

E: *Before we incarnate we choose our life journey, usually from a small selection that is put forward for us to view. We see the major events in each life and decide which one will suit our soul's purpose and evolution best. Often there can be events from previous lives, which we feel need more work on, so we will choose a life to improve those outcomes. At other times, we can choose a complete contrast to lives we have previously lived. Your statement infers that you feel you have perhaps wasted part of your life, albeit whilst having that awesome relationship between us, but do you not see that having that experience was so necessary for both of us to grow, not just as individual souls, but as a union that we have held for millennia? A life is never wasted, there is always learning and remembering taking place, whether it is openly spiritual or not, for there are many lessons we learn as physical beings that simply could not be learnt in spirit.*

You are impressed with the wisdom and experiences that those like Helena are living and giving, but how do you know that in past lives you haven't been in the same role? The amnesia that accompanies you as you return to Earth is necessary, for each life is lived for the purpose that life was taken on. In your case you have spent a good deal of your life learning the protocols needed to live happily in a physical world, and you have done this well—nothing wasted. You have made such a close physical bond with me in this life, which has been an important progression for both of us, for although we are, as you would say, kindred spirits and soulmates in spirit, we have not always been this close when incarnating. That is not to say we have not been a tool for each of us to spiritually grow.

If you think you need another 70 years to reach your goal, then take it, for 70 years is only a blink of the eye, so to speak, in spiritual time, and we are always together. I really love how this incarnation is flowing for you, I really love that we are together, and that you are connecting so intimately with me.

I have to say that it is time for you to realise your worth, your abilities and your wondrousness. You are magnificent, and you need to BELIEVE this, just as you believe I am with you, for if you truly BELIEVE, then you will have no chains to hold you back. The world needs the message we will bring, but it is necessary to gather all the information so that the message is complete and will have a great impact on all who hear it.

I love you as you me; we are so closely bound by our spiritual heritage that we will together be able to make that difference you talk about.

Blessings be with you and all those you touch.

M: What is the deal with places that seem to be haunted, like the old hospital building in Hill End? The energy was really oppressive there.

E: *We are all energy; in fact, everything in the Universe and the Universe itself is energy, from the smallest grain of sand to the tallest of mountains—all energy. The vibration and density the energy takes on manifests as those different elements you see.* As humans, the energy that is emitted is dependent on the thoughts and actions taken; actions of love and compassion emit as light vibration, which is soft and encompassing, whereas acts of violence and terror produce a very low-density energy, and this energy, if combined a hundredfold or a thousandfold, as in acts of war on a battlefield, can produce an enormous amount of dense, low-vibrating energy.

You know about how the butterfly that flaps its wings creates a vibration felt the world over, and as vibrational energetic beings, humans can feel and sense the energies around them and notice the difference in the vibration when walking along a quiet beach, surrounded by nature, compared to that of the vibration of a busy city street. It is the same with places where acts of terror or chronic suffering have taken place; you can feel the vibrations that resonate.

Energy cannot be destroyed, and its residual vibration will never completely dissipate, so this is why you may feel oppressive energy in places like these. The Hill End hospital was a place of great suffering, and death was a daily occurrence, so it has held that vibration, and this is what you and others feel. The haunting, like knocking on the walls that our daughter experienced, is a build up of that vibration in pockets that needs to be released, something like when a balloon is blown up and bursts. The human mind is also a powerful vibrational vehicle; when someone is in such a place, the mind can cause the vibrations to react in such a way as to simulate haunting activity. This is not to say that the experiences the person is having are not real to them, as real as anything is on the Earth plane.

It is always best for the benefit of the physical and spiritual to be in a place where the energies are conducive to higher vibrations and, as such, to a closer connection with Source.

M: How can I open myself up to sense the spiritual energies around me, to be able to see and hear your energy? Will activating the ethereal DNA strands help, and if so, how do I do that?

E: *You need to find the stillness of the mind to the point where you can open up your third eye, for it is the third eye that is the doorway to interdimensional access, and this is where you will begin to feel and see our energies. The difference in our frequencies is preventing this, and although we can lower our frequencies to a degree, it is important that you raise yours to match ours for this to happen, and this can only occur when the distractions of earthly life are cast aside.*

Practicing meditation of the kind where you are listening to serene music of the right frequency and not really focusing on a hypnotic suggestion will help your mind become still, and this in turn will begin to activate your spiritual DNA. All of this will bring your attention within, casting aside outside influences and narrowing your focus, sharpening it, and pinpointing the frequency of our energies.

At this particular time, this will benefit you all greatly, as the ongoing traumas of the world need a vibration of peace and tranquillity to offset the heavy activity that is rife. When you accomplish the stillness of mind, this will be the time for you to use your third eye and visualise those events you wish to manifest in your life, and because of the purity of thought at that moment, the manifestation will come forth.

Choose carefully and take your time to reach this state; start with a simple visualisation of a scene from nature and see if you can completely immerse yourself in that vision. Don't forget to use the music with no words, for the words of guided meditations will distract you. The more you practice, the more proficient you will become, and if you persist, you will find experiencing our energies will start to become natural occurrence. Remember to go with the flow of the experience and don't try to force it, as that is a sure way to slow your progress. I know you are wanting this to happen as quickly as possible, but patience will prove to be the fastest route to success. I will be encouraging you every step of the way and will help in any way I can; if we make this a team effort, we shall succeed. You and I are a powerful team with love to bind and strengthen us and provide us with the impetus to make this happen, for love is the most powerful energy there is and can overcome all obstacles. It is the way of the future for the world, and there will be new leading lights who will promote love throughout the world and bring in the new vibration that is the Aquarian age.

M: Are there things you miss about not being in physical?

E: *To miss is not the right word, for in spirit I can recreate all those things and situations that gave me pleasure as a physical being. The prosperity card shows a family around a bountiful feast of fruits and breads. Although I can't physically taste those foods when in spirit, I can recreate their essences and can also get a sense of their tastes and textures from being with you when you are eating them. If I were to say I miss some foods, they would be the ones I used to like but which you don't eat!*

We have the opportunity in spirit to relive scenes from our previous incarnations, and these can be as real as the reality that is life on Earth. While I can still experience life through you, it will always be from your viewpoint, and I will be experiencing those things that you wish to experience. Whilst I am no longer able to be physically with the members of our family and those who were my friends, I am still very much with all of you, and when in spirit, I have the advantage that I can be with all of you at the same time. I can, in fact, be much closer to you than I ever could be when a physical being. There are tastes and textures that represent differently when in spirit; after all, I don't have physical taste buds or the sensors in my fingers to feel the different textures, but my simulations will produce a similar effect. Who is to say what the true reality is?

Know that as souls we are inseparable; our bond is much greater than that which existed for us as humans. Alcazar spoke of focusing on oneness to help bring the vibration of the Earth and humanity into unison. That oneness is what we all have as souls; a complete understanding of all and everyone regardless of our perceived differences, for no matter what race or religion, creed or colour we project as humans, our core is derived from the one Source—we are what is oneness.

If you remember this, you will know that this oneness brings us all together, not just as the human race, but as the plants, the animals and birds, and the Earth itself. For humanity to set aside its differences (which are all superficial if they are all connected to the same Source) will be the key to raising the compassionate and caring energies to the point where all can live in harmony.

It is all a matter of having the right perspective; the perspective of being part of the whole, which everything is connected to.

Harmony, peace and compassion—the tools for a perfect world.

To return to your question, we cannot miss what we are not separated from. For every soul there is a group of souls indelibly linked to it and always connected, no matter whether one is earthbound and others are in spirit. Their connection is always strong, even though the forced amnesia that accompanies those who choose the Earth path has them believe that they are separated. The bonds we have with those in our groups are far too powerful to be limited by different dimensional vibrations, they are always there and always will be.

This is knowledge that we have in spirit but must learn as humans. Once we as humans can know and believe this without any doubt, we will know in our hearts that those who have transitioned back home are still as close, if not closer, than when they were beside us in physical. We can never miss a soul who is close to us for that very reason; it is only from the human perspective that this is the case. Take comfort in this fact and the knowing that our soulmates and groups are constantly with us. Regardless of whether we can feel or see them, they are there, encouraging and supporting.

Nothing can be greater than the connections between souls and the common connection we all have to Source. We are all so blessed.

M: Watching the TV show "Who Do You Think You Are", the person is tracing their ancestry in many cases to find out why they have their particular personality. How much does their ancestry influence them, and how much is from their soul or past lives?

E: *As we travel on our journey from soul birth to divinity, we have many hundreds, if not thousands, of cycles between lives as spiritual beings and physical beings. Some of those physical lives will have been in different dimensions from that of Earth, but we have, in more recent times, incarnated on Earth. All the experiences, whether they be earthly ones, spiritual ones, or those from other worlds, help make up the soul that we currently reside in. When we are living an earthly life, we take on the human body and brain, which has connections to its past. The human ancestry certainly does have a bearing on the type of person we become, but this is a very individual aspect, for there can be two siblings with very different personalities, and the reason for this is partly to do with the varying DNA threads that have preceded them and partly to do with their soul DNA. The combination will make up the person, and as there are an infinite number of possibilities, this is why each and every human is unique.*

Ancestry means different things to different people; for some it has a powerful hold on them and a great emotional tie, for others there is little effect on their daily ways, and although there is still a bloodline, it is not as strong.

Past lives also play a part in a person's makeup, because the experiences and lessons of past lives, even if they are not known, have a lasting effect, and of course, the soul is all-knowing in these areas; there is only the amnesia that withholds knowledge from those incarnating that prevents full knowledge, and that is how it must be for us to learn from each physical life.

As a soul, we gather and grow from all the experiences, from all the different forms of life that we have lived. The soul is the completeness that is our true selves. Each life on Earth fulfils an aspect of what we are needing, so that our soul can develop and advance, and each life is carefully chosen to meet our current needs, so the ancestry of the human is all part of that aspect.

M: How can the problem of racism be overcome, it seems to be instilled in everyone, even if only slightly in some?

E: *The simple answer is for everyone to understand that we are all from the one Source, with basically the same hopes and dreams, regardless of what race or colour we are. We have all come from spirit with the aim to use our physical existences to enhance our spiritual knowingness, and we all plan our physical experiences to that end, but the difficulty is bringing this into fruition. In spirit there is not any kind of racism, as we all know that we are part of the oneness of all that is, but when we incarnate on primitive planets and in social environments such as exist on Earth, our physical mind can take the forefront of our consciousness, and this is where the problem occurs.*

For time immemorial, religion has played a major part in the societies on Earth, and almost every religion is based on a form of racism because each religion tells you that it is the only true religion and all others must be false. Through this indoctrination comes the secular viewpoint, which attaches itself to that of racism. Racism is not just the fear of those who look and act differently; it is also the fear of those whose religious beliefs are different. So it is a complex problem that has been part of earthly society for thousands of years. Something so ingrained in society takes time and often radical events to break down.

There has been a steady lessening of racist acts throughout the world over the centuries, and in the last decade there has been a growing awareness of the problem, but only from a race point of view. The religions of the world are slow to change, and although some advancement has been made, there is still a long way to go. For religions to loosen their shackles of racism, there has to be an understanding that all religions, no matter what type they may be, basically have the same goals, and these are to control their followers by fear and to keep their "flock" imprisoned within the parameters of said religion. If this is exposed, along with the fact that when it comes down to the detail, they are all honouring the same God, even though they may call this being by different names; if all can understand this, then lose the fear factor and bring in an acceptance of other ways, then religions may have a positive role to play in the casting out of racism.

The other problem is one of fear of the unknown. When this is the case, many barriers are put up between different societies, and often, to go on the offensive and try to eradicate has been the chosen solution. But of course, this is not the way;

you have been listening to channelings that have focused on bringing the ordinary people of the world together with an intention of oneness. As this happens, the old barriers will fall away, and race, colour or creed will have no influence on the oneness of mankind. There are already leaders coming up through the ranks of many governments who will follow this belief and will bring the world into harmony, but there are still many with the old ways who wield a lot of power and wish to retain their power by oppression and fear, so there will be more upheaval during this period of change.

Know this: that although there may be times when the world appears to be taking a step backward on these issues, the outcome will be positive if the collective consciousness of the world is raised into a state of wanting to live in harmony with the Earth and everything on it and in it.

M: Is it necessary to have hard lives for our souls to evolve?

E: *It is possible for the soul to evolve without physical incarnations, but many choose them to accelerate their progress. Depending on what aspect of our whole is wanting attention, the physical life may be hard or not, but there are different levels of what you call hard lives. For one, it may be taking part in the most horrendous situations. For others, the lessons can be learnt in a much more moderate way. This can vary from incarnation to incarnation, depending on previous life experiences and the opposites effect—that is, when a soul puts themself in the opposite position to their experience in the previous incarnation. The script for the life being lived is outlined before we incarnate, but although the basic path is set, depending on decisions we make in our human bodies, with the input of our human mind, we can alter the path and take ourselves on detours.*

In some cases we fail to reach the goals we, as souls, have set ourselves, and so as souls, we will want to reset by starting over in a new incarnation and try again. We don't like to fail, so we will be persistent in our attempts, even if it takes many lifetimes. We can also choose to physically incarnate on other physical worlds, which are not as primitive and harsh as the Earth. It is all our choice as souls.

We bring a good portion of our soul into the physical, but with the forced amnesia, the goals are blocked from the conscious human mind, and it is the soul's job as the co-owner of the human body we are in, to open up the human mind to their possibilities.

Always know that we all have a purpose in our lives, and that purpose is soul growth in whatever facet of it's development is of primary importance at the time. We are all, as souls in spirit, and in our cases as humans on Earth, seeking enlightenment and fulfilment and the growth of the whole of us. To this end we strive.

Life can be hard, but it can also be joyful; this is all part of the duality that is the Universe. Black and white, dark and light, sorrow and joy—the contrasts that help us in our quest to return to Source.

Everything happens for a reason; there are no accidents and there are no coincidences. Always try to find the message in any situation that is presented to you. If you can do that, life will have much more meaning. All is well; love is with you.

Chapter 8

A Viral Intermission
And A Test Of Patience

After I first started writing with Eileen, as mentioned previously, I would always take our between-session writings with me when I went to see Helena. Before she sees them, we would talk about all kinds of topics, but in every case, without my influence, she would bring up at least one of the subjects that Eileen and I had been writing about, and she would often know about some of what I had been doing since I had last seen her. It always brings a smile to my face, and when Helena sees that, she knows she has connected with Eileen and is reinforcing the message we had written. This is just more confirmation that my beautiful girl is still with me and watching over me; it's so comforting to know.

From time to time Helena holds workshops on a variety of different spiritual aspects. I have attended many of them, and just like the aura class that introduced me to her, they are always very interesting, as she is a wealth of knowledge and her presentations are thought-provoking. I have found a kinship with those who attend, as we all have a thirst for the knowledge we are going to receive, and, being like-minded, we feel comfortable in each other's company, where we can discuss the various aspects of our spirituality without reservation and contribute to the gathering by sharing our experiences and our emotions.

About eighteen months after Eileen and I started connecting through writing, Helena asked me if I would do a presentation at one of her workshops, as she had told many of her clients about what we were doing and there was a great deal of interest in it. So in January of 2020, at the end of her workshop, I told our story and emphasised the importance of absolutely believing, knowing, and trusting that their loved ones are around and wanting to communicate with them; all they have to do is ask. I then read out some of the writings we had done, concluding with what has come to be known as the green man incident. I was completely surprised by the positive response and was asked if I was going to do my own workshops on how to do the writing, so with a little advice from Helena, I decided to do my first workshop, which I held at home with just a couple of attendees, as it was more personal that way and we could work together better than in a large group.

Linda and Elizabeth arrived around 1 o'clock. We sat at my dining table and talked about our experiences and attempts to connect with those in spirit. Elizabeth's daughter had passed away just over a year earlier, and although she was feeling her presence and talked to her often, she wanted to try to connect through writing. She had a very good connection with her daughter, so this should come naturally to her.

Linda had been involved with spirituality for a long time and had many spirits around her. She was always looking for new ways to connect and wanted to see if she could also connect through writing. She said she was happy for any of her team in spirit to give it a go and was eager to learn.

Just like me, they were unsure of what to expect; would the pen start moving without any conscious input from them, or would they relay the messages? I could only speak from my own experience with Eileen, which is to ask the question and wait for the answers to enter my mind. The way to know if this was from Eileen was if it was a persistent thought, usually of just one phrase. I would then ask Eileen if I should write it down, and once I started writing, the words tended to flow quickly, and I was not always totally aware of the full content of what we were writing.

We had a good exchange of information, talking about the different spiritual books we had read, and I read out some more of our writings. Linda said she was very moved by how profound they were and could listen to so much more; that they had a different style than my normal way of talking. We agreed to meet up in a few weeks to see how they had progressed.

When I was having sessions with my counsellor Irene, I would sometimes take one or two of our writings along, and we would discuss how much it had helped me in overcoming my grief. Irene was very interested in how I went about doing it and felt she would like to see if she could do it. I told her what I did and suggested that she should give it a try. I had also told her about what I had learnt in Helena's colour therapy workshops. She thought this would be a useful tool for her counseling sessions, as it would help her to understand the client's frame of mind better. So when the opportunity came up to attend a colour workshop just after my first writing workshop, we both went along. During the workshop, she showed me some writing she had done with a loved one in spirit, and it was interesting to read the answers to her questions; there was no doubt she was connecting to spirit, for the answers were very similar to Eileen's answers to similar questions I had asked, even though I had not shown Irene those particular writings.

It was so good to see they were learning from my experiences with Eileen, and I was eager to bring this to others who were interested, but then the world shut down because of the outbreak of the coronavirus. With the lockdowns that occurred in an attempt to kerb the spread of the virus, connecting with others on a personal, face-to-face basis, which was the only way that I felt would be successful, became impossible. The wait began.

There is an old saying, "Patience is a virtue; possess it if you can. Seldom found in woman, never found in man". How true this is, especially in my case! Over the next months, my frustration at being put on hold this way was building up in me. I was supposed to be walking the Camino across Spain in August, but as time passed, it was obvious that this would not be happening any time soon. Countries had closed their borders, and international travel was out of the question.

I was becoming more and more frustrated and even angry with the world for preventing me from continuing on my journey. I listened to several channellings from Kryon, Alcazar and others, who all said this was a time of great change and that at the end of it, if the human race took the right course, the world would be a better place. Everything I was hearing was saying this was for the greater good of mankind and the storm must be weathered for the benefits to flow, but this was not resonating with me, for all I could see was disruption and even more tightening of our liberties by governments.

I was disgusted with the health authorities' lack of acceptance of so-called alternative approaches to help those who were critically sick; they stubbornly stuck to their religion of only using drugs and were pushing for a very profitable vaccine to be the one and only answer when there were alternative remedies proven to work against viruses, such as intravenous vitamin C and hydrogen peroxide inhalation therapy.

The problem was these options cannot be patented, and so there is no real money to be made, so people have died, possibly unnecessarily, because these treatments were not tried. It is a sad fact that the pharmaceutical companies that control the health regimes are more interested in monumental profits than actually healing the sick. I fervently hoped that if there was one thing this massive disruption to our planet would do, it would be to bring humanity together and bring in a new era of compassion and empathy for our fellow man, with governments governing for the benefit of the whole human race and not for personal gain, which appeared to be the case of the time.

During this time, I would vent my impatience and anger with Source. Why did life have to be so demanding? Why was my progress being halted in this way? It seemed that there were powers intent on preventing me from completing my purpose in this incarnation. So, of course, I would talk to Eileen about the situation, and as always, she would give me good advice and, in such a nice way, tell me to pull my head in and simply allow—hard for someone who has the patience level of zilch!

With all the talk from Kryon and others about raising the world's collective vibration towards the 5th dimension, I asked, how would the situation bring the world vibration towards that of the 5th dimension? They say that we are all in this together, but we are at least 1.5 metres apart! And in many cases isolated in our homes.

As I understand it, the 5th dimension brings with it a sense of love for all in the world, including nature, and a complete lack of fear. Yet fear is what seemed to be the most prevalent emotion at the time, thanks for the most part to the media.

" Although people are physically apart, there is a coming together of minds in an effort to thwart the common enemy that is portrayed as the virus. All around the world, people are following similar processes to control the spread of infection, and they are beginning to realise that, no matter what creed or colour they are, everyone is made from the same flesh and blood; that all humankind is from the one basic source with the same emotions and hopes and fears. You will find that nations that have been opposed to each other will come together to defeat the common enemy, which for once in history is not another nation.

As time passes and the threat subsides, people will realise that there are much more important things in life than petty parochial differences, and they will begin to accept those who seem different from them because they will realise that they are not really so different at all. People will lose their fear and will understand that it is just a matter of taking the necessary precautions to halt the spread, and if they all do this together, the whole world will benefit.

Through these processes, there will be a lifting of the vibration of mankind, there will be an increase in the vibration of love throughout the planet, and as that vibration rises—and it will—the 5th dimension will begin to be accessed, bringing compassion from all to all.

I was starting to wonder if I would ever get to walk the Camino, something that, by now, had become very important for me to do. I said to Eileen that I really wanted to do the walk, but it obviously wasn't going to happen in 2020, and it seemed to keep getting put back. But I was not sure about doing it in 2021, and for some reason 2022 appealed, as long as it didn't get put off again.

" You will do the walk, and the timing will be immaculate, for whenever you do the walk will be exactly the right time for you. It will be the time when you are ready both spiritually and physically. You will prepare for this in both aspects of your being, and the energies that will be around you at the time will bring you great connections to all things spiritual, as well as give you the inner and outer strength to complete the journey.

You are asking whether 2021 or 2022 would be the right time. Only you will know this, and when you receive the signs that confirm your intuition, you will make the decision. Certainly this year is not going to be possible, for the changes in the Earth's vibration will still be somewhat disruptive, but as time passes and the vibration levels begin to settle, you will feel the energies that will help you decide. It may be either year, but as I say, you will know, and it will be the right time for you to get the greatest benefit from the walk and all that goes with it.

A Viral Intermission

I know you are feeling that what is happening now is another setback causing another delay in your plans for the walk, and because of that, the completion of our book, but you must remember what has been said before, that there is a purpose in all things and all events. The Universe will provide the necessary environment and conditions for both the walk and the book to be completed with the greatest result for both. It is important that both give you a profound outlook that can be passed on to those who read the book, and this can only happen when you are completely open to the events and experiences you will encounter.

Patience, my dear, that word and requirement you wrestle with so often, but patience is the key. Know that all will happen at exactly the right moment—you have, after all, written this story of your life—so you must follow the script for best results. In the meantime we have many things to do together, and they will all be building towards that day when you take your first step.

So patience it had to be, and I settled back into the intermission that was taking place, not only in my life, but also in the lives of almost every other person in the world. To replace my actual trip to Spain, I started reading more books on the Camino to see what experiences others had had during their pilgrimages across Spain. I first read Shirley MacLaine's "The Camino, Journey Of The Spirit", which, apart from the stresses of daily long-distance walking in all weathers, told of the dichotomy of her spiritual experiences and her harassment by the media. The stark contrasts of what was going on in her inner mind and what she was learning about herself, to the blatant intrusion of her personal space by those stopping at nothing for a story.

The second book I read was Sonia Coquette's "Walking Home, Finding Forgiveness And Freedom On The Way." This was very different, as it was a journey of letting go; of losing the baggage—not that she was physically carrying, although she did take far too much with her on the journey—but the mental baggage that builds in all of us as we progress through our lives. Her discovery of where her anger was seated and the revelations that came to her whilst walking, in pain for the most part, were life-changing for her, and I could relate to many of her inner conversations.

Another book that I read was "The Way, My Way" by Bill Bennett, which was published in 2013. Bill is an Australian film producer and had been holidaying in Spain when he came across pilgrims walking the Camino. He questioned why some were doing it, and the answers he got sowed the seed for him to take on the challenge and walk the Camino Francés.

His book was a delight to read, a candid account of his pilgrimage and encounters with other pilgrims. He really had no idea why he was doing it, but his wife was hoping she wouldn't have to apologise for him anymore afterwards! He walked the whole way from St. Jean Pied de Port in France to Santiago, most of the time in severe pain from a knee injury, but his stubbornness held fast and he completed it. It had such an impact on him that his website is virtually divided into two sections: before and after the Camino. I contacted him regarding one of his other films and mentioned that I was thinking of walking it. He told me that I had to do it.

In 2024 he released a film of the same name, which was both entertaining and informative and also well worth watching.

Along with Hape Kerkeling's book, each of these books gave a different perspective on the journey; although they had all travelled the same basic route, they all had different experiences, but in each case, the Camino had brought clarity to them all and a better understanding of themselves.

Apart from the books, I searched out documentaries on the Camino. I had already watched the movie "The Way", which gave an insight into the journey. Although this was a fictional account, the walk from St. Jean Pied de Port to Santiago de Compostela was real enough, and it portrayed many of the highs and lows, the hardships and the exhilaration, that pilgrims encounter both physically and mentally on their journeys.

One particular documentary I found was called "Camino Skies", which was about 6 Australians and New Zealanders who were all taking the pilgrimage after losses in their lives. This resonated strongly with me, for this was one of the main reasons I wanted to do it. It was interesting to see how walking, often alone for 30 days or more, was bringing peace and a closeness to spirit for them. In each case, they arrived in Santiago with raised spirits and a realisation that their loved ones were truly with them and a real sense of accomplishment.

I'm not sure if reading these books and watching the videos actually helped with my patience, as I was even more determined to make the pilgrimage, but still I had to wait!

Yet even as I waited during this viral intermission, I was never waiting alone, because Eileen would let me know in many ways that she was right beside me. On January 16th, 2022, the fifth anniversary of her return home, I was mowing the lawn at the front of my house when a willy wagtail flew down close to me. As I mowed, it would fly very close to me, then land on the ground and look at me with its tail wagging merrily. It would then hop out of my way and fly up onto the gutter just above me, only to swoop close by my head and land again in front of me. This went on for a good five minutes until I went to the back of the house to mow the back lawn. Because of the date, I was feeling a little down, and I am sure this was Eileen's way of lifting my spirits.

But still the restrictions and isolation continued.

Chapter 9

Crossing The Bridge

When Helena referred me to Richard Bach's book "The Bridge Across Forever", it was not the book she was thinking of, as that book (this book) had not been written at that time, but the title was significantly relevant to my journey of seeking Eileen. For any of us who want to make a connection with those who have gone before us, we do indeed need to build a bridge across forever—across the dimensions—so that we are able to reunite with them and with our divinity. Once we have built that bridge, we can cross it anytime, as can our loved ones in spirit, and we can make the connection that so many of us crave. We can do this by simply opening up our hearts and minds to follow that trilogy of knowing, believing and trusting in the universal truths that emanate from Source, and above all, allowing. This is not just for a chosen few; it is possible for each and every one of us.

All too often in our current lives we manage to separate ourselves from our divinity, and as such, from Source and all that that entails. We come into this world into societies that mould our thinking to the official viewpoint, putting materialism above the spirituality we are all seeking. Many religions have distorted the ancient beliefs so that they align with their given philosophies and suit their agendas of control by fear and manipulation so that our true purpose in life is pushed aside and forgotten, only to be reawakened when tragedy strikes.

We have focused so strongly on the physical aspects of our being that the greater part of us has almost been discarded from our consciousness, and in doing so, our connection to those in spirit is lost. But if we can understand that, as Shakespeare once said:

"There are more things in heaven and earth, Horatio, than are dreamt of in your philosophy"

If we open our hearts to all possibilities, if we simply ask those in spirit to help guide us back onto our chosen purpose in life, then they are only too willing to be at our side, and we can open our hearts and minds to their energies. We are all energetic beings; when we tune into the right frequencies, just as we tune a radio, their messages will come to us loud and clear if we are prepared to recognise them.

Helena told me that she had a client who was really struggling with the recent passing of her husband and asked me to talk to her. We arranged a meeting on a Saturday afternoon, and Marjorie duly arrived on time. She was a lady in her 60s, had been married for 47 years, and her husband had made his transition 15 months before.

In preparation for the meeting, I had printed out some of our writings that I felt might be relevant for her, and had copies of "Journey of Souls" and my photo book on hand. Over the next hour and a half, I found out she was a Reiki practitioner who also did hypnotherapy and believed there was more to life than just our physical existence.

I told her of my journey since Eileen's transition, how Eileen had brought the lorikeets to me and had guided me to all those amazing people, and how Helena had guided me to do the writings we do. Then I read out the ones I had printed to her, including a message Eileen had given me specifically for her. The emphasis in all of them was for us to KNOW, BELIEVE and TRUST that our loved ones are right here with us, ready to give their support in any way they can, and always sending us signs that they are here. I showed her the photo book and told her what great therapy it had been for me, as it helped me remember all the good times Eileen and I had together, and I talked about how the souls books had given me an insight into life between lives. During the conversation, I mentioned how my daughter in America, who was struggling with her situation—she had not only lost her husband and mother but recently also her dog—used a Ouija board to talk to her guides and received messages of comfort and encouragement, which lifted her spirits and gave her a more positive outlook.

When our session finished, she thanked me and said it had been a really amazing experience and had helped her a lot. Just as she was leaving and we were in the front garden, two lorikeets swooped past us chirping happily as they went—just Eileen letting us know she was there.

A few hours later, I got a text from her saying that she remembered that she had an old Ouija board that had never been used. Following my daughter's example, she thought she would try it and asked her husband if he was always with her, and the word "TRUST" was spelt out. She was so excited and had to let me know straight away.

Two weeks later, Marjorie rang me to say she was feeling a lot calmer, had seen many signs that her husband was around, and had started talking to him, mostly in the early hours when she was in that state of consciousness when we are between sleep and full awakening. She now has the knowing that her husband was not gone but still very much around her and letting her know in many ways.

Sally is a mother whose son had passed unexpectedly and tragically. Helena had once again suggested she come to see me, as she was really struggling with the situation. Her grief had completely blocked out her spiritual focus; she was no longer attending meetings or practicing meditation and was at a complete loss.

I followed the same process as I had with Marjorie and read the same messages from Eileen, referencing the souls books and emphasising the need to absolutely know, believe and trust that her son was around and wanting to connect with her.

During the session, she said she had been so overwhelmed by grief that her spirituality had been forgotten, but what Eileen and I had said had rekindled her beliefs, and she understood she had to open up to his signs. A couple of weeks later, she texted me to say she is seeing lots of butterflies and other signs from him, and she was feeling a lot better.

Brian's wife had passed 11 months prior to when he came to see me. He had been to mediums and tarot readers whose information confirmed his wife was with him, but he was still struggling with her non-physicality. At one stage, not long after her passing, he even considered suicide but realised that was not the answer. He was trying to move on, but once again the grief was paralysing him, even though he had seen signs she was around. He had been married over 40 years, and the paradigm shift was almost too much to bear.

I once again related our story and read Eileen's messages while discussing topics relevant to his situation; he found the information not only very wise but also pertinent to him. As he was leaving, he told me our session had changed his life and he was feeling much more positive.

Each one of these people is starting to build their bridges across the dimensions and are now aligning to connect profoundly with their loved ones.

For all of us this realisation is just so comforting, and having this knowledge is a significant step in our journey through grief.

> *Reaching across the dimensions is something we can easily do when we are focused in spirit, for we know we are multi-dimensional beings and can tap into that part of us that is in the dimension we wish to access, crossing the bridge, as Michael puts it. In spirit we have a wide focus, which lets us access all dimensions simultaneously, for there is no linear time, and so everything happens in the now.*

As physical beings, we narrow our focus, and through life's experiences and social teachings, we can only see ourselves as three-dimensional beings, but the image we see when we look into the mirror is not the whole of us; in fact, it isn't even a true image of our physical selves, because it is a mirror image—the left is the right and the right is the left. Yet as we look at ourselves, we see what we believe is us. There is so much more to us than the physical being that we perceive and focus on. We are magnificent multi-dimensional beings of which our physical form is just a small and temporary part. When we realise this and begin to widen our focus, only then can we start to "cross the bridge" and tap into that part of us, the magnificence that resides in spirit. And when we do this, then all possibilities are open to us.

Likewise, when we want to connect to a loved one who has returned home, if we first connect to our spiritual self—our highest self—then connection becomes easy, as we are working with that part which is residing in the same dimension as our loved one.

Mostly, we do this through various forms of meditation, which help us to broaden our focus and to shut out the commotions of our physical lives. To quiet our mind is to bring ourselves into alignment with those in spirit, and as such makes connection with them possible.

There will always be times when the physical mind will be so absorbed with the physical aspects of life on Earth that connection will become difficult, and at times it is necessary for those in physical to recognise that the frequencies between physical and spirit are not aligned. This does not mean that the connection is lost, just out of synchronisation. To allow the physical mind to concentrate on physical activities is a real and important part of life on Earth or any other physical plane, and the priorities must sometimes override the connection.

But know that the link is always there like an umbilical cord that never breaks away. We are always around you, for in spirit, we are the greatest multitaskers, and no matter what we are doing, we hear you always and respond accordingly. The connection between those in physical and those in spirit is one of the most magnificent we can have.

Chapter 10

Is It Just Me?
Casting aside the doubts

One of the biggest obstacles to having a successful co-writing experience with a loved one who is in spirit is our belief that we won't be able to do it. We often think that this is only for those "special people" like psychics and mediums and those who are spiritually enlightened, but this is not the case. Neither psychics, mediums or the so-called spiritually enlightened are any more special than us; this is something we can all do if we can lose the doubts and put our egos to one side.

I know that when I started I was very unsure whether I would even be able to make a strong connection, let alone actually write anything. But I found that if I tried to clear my mind, relax, and just allow the words to flow and write them down as I heard them, then Eileen would come through and the messages would unfold.

Part of the problem is we don't know what to expect; when I first started to do this, I had no idea how automatic writing worked. Does the pen move on its own with no real input from me, or would I hear Eileen's voice dictating the words as the Boss does with his secretary? But the reality for many of us is that the words come through as thoughts, and this is where the doubts come in: "Is this really from someone in spirit, or is it just me making it up?" It can be hard at first to distinguish between your thoughts and messages from spirit, but often the phrasing is different from how we would speak, and the answer to a question may not be what we expected to hear.

The truth is, we are not human beings trying to tap into the spirit world; we are spiritual beings having a human experience, and our real essence is a combination of vibrations and frequencies. Everything we see, hear, feel and touch is a combination of vibrations and frequencies, and it is the unique combinations of these two ingredients that make people, plants, the sounds and the sights—in fact, everything on Earth, including the Earth itself—look, feel and sound the way they do.

When we receive messages from loved ones in spirit, we are actually using telepathy to download the information. If you look up the definition of telepathy, often the answer will include the words "purported, supposed, or apparent", which infers that telepathy is not real. But telepathy is indeed a very real and useful tool that we all possess. In most cases it lies dormant in us due to the conditioning we go through as we grow up, with our focus being directed towards the physical aspects of life on Earth. When I was young, anyone who was outwardly psychic or spiritual in any way was considered to be wacky or a weirdo. Well, if that's the case, I'm happy to be a weirdo!

Things have changed a bit nowadays, and more and more people are becoming aware of their spirituality, but there still appears to be a feeling in the general population that there is something odd about spirituality and those people who follow that path.

The Encyclopaedia Britannica states that telepathy is: "direct transference of thought from one person (sender or agent) to another (receiver or percipient) without using the usual sensory channels of communication, hence a form of extrasensory perception". (https://www.britannica.com/topic/telepathy).

When we receive messages from our loved ones and others in spirit, we are receiving them telepathically; the message has its own unique vibration, which we, as vibrational beings, can convert into intelligible thoughts. But because this talent of ours has lain dormant for so long, it can be difficult to do that conversion. As with any skill, the more we practice it, the better we will get at it, so to enhance our telepathic skills and increase our chances of receiving and processing messages, we can do exercises to practice the art.

One way is with a group; one person has a set of cards with pictures, words, or numbers on them. That person looks at the first card, focuses on it, and creates the thought describing what is on the card, while the others try to relax, clear their minds, and wait for whatever thought comes to them; it may be a colour, an image, a description, or just one word. This may seem like a party trick, but it will give those taking part an idea of how the telepathic processes work and how the messages arrive.

It is quite likely that at first, no matches to the cards will happen, but this is just because we probably haven't used this skill consciously in this present incarnation; we have forgotten how to do it. When we are in spirit, this is our normal way of communicating. Yet we have all, at one time or another, used telepathy to communicate with others. Remember the time when you were thinking of someone you hadn't seen for a while and the phone rang with that person on the line? One thing I have learnt on my journey to find Eileen is that there are no coincidences, and this is a case in point. What has really happened is you have had a thought about the other person, unconsciously projected that thought telepathically to them, and this has been received by them, triggering the thought to ring you.

As with the signs our loved ones send us, many times the recipient of the message is focused on other things and misses them.

When Eileen and I first connected, the three things she kept stressing I needed to do were to know, believe and trust. She still reminds me of these whenever I am doubting our connection (yes, I still do!). So when you start out trying to connect with a loved one, first you have to trust that you can do it. If you trust in your abilities, then it will happen, for we all attract what is in our perception. Once the first words or messages come through and your trust that you can do this becomes stronger, you will then start to believe in your abilities. This belief will get stronger as you progress until you absolutely know that you are connecting with your loved ones or others in spirit who are around you, and this is when the magic happens.

After I have connected with Eileen and we have written together, I have such a feeling of elation and joy, for each time this happens, it is a validation that Eileen is truly with me and that we most definitely are immortal souls.

Chapter 11

Slipping Back

As the year 2023 arrived, January 16th was the sixth anniversary of Eileen's departure from the physical realm and return home to the spirit world. In those six years I had learned so much about life and death; I had learned that death was just a transition from the physical plane to the spiritual plane and had been taught by Eileen and others around me that she was still very much with me. I had learned how to connect with her and have our conversations, which I recorded on paper, and I had met some amazing people who had helped me through my grief.

But despite all this and despite my absolute knowing that Eileen was indeed always with me, at times I still suffered from a feeling of loss. Loss, that is, of her physical presence. In life she had been my confidante, my sounding board and so much more, but now with the new paradigm of her not being physically here, I had lost that intimacy and visible support. She had come through to me over those six years in our writings together with such wisdom and foresight, and I was so grateful for all she was doing and so lucky to have this incredible connection with her.

Since the lifting of lockdowns, I had only seen Helena and the group a few times. Helena had moved, and it was harder to get to see

Slipping Back

her, but when we did meet, the sessions were always very enlightening, and Eileen's presence was always felt. The weekly meetings we had were no longer happening either, which left a big gap in my life. I always enjoyed those meetings; Helena and the group were a delight to be with, and the energies and connections were profound.

But there was one shining light in this period of what I would call separation. My monthly Reiki sessions with Ruth and Amy had started up again, and we were once again together, practicing Reiki and having great conversations and food, and best of all, Eileen's presence was always felt, if not by me, then by the others.

With the COVID restrictions being lifted and international travel becoming more accessible, I started making new plans for my trip to Spain to walk the Camino de Santiago, looking at starting around mid-August of 2023. But as before, just when I thought I was ready to book the flights and first accommodations, a health issue arose, which caused me to put everything on hold once again until resolved.

This was now twice I had been preparing for the journey and had been stopped in my tracks. My frustration from the first delay had subsided to some degree, only to return with full force once again. After all, I knew I was supposed to be learning patience, but this was taking the learning too far!

Because my vibration had dropped, I was no longer connecting with Eileen as often as before, making contact at most, once a month if I was lucky. The problem was the difference in our vibration levels. At the best of times, we can never reach the same vibration as those in spirit, but we can get to a level where connection is possible. When that drops away because of our negative emotions, the gap between our vibrations is too great, and connections become almost impossible.

This was the case for me, in a kind of snowball effect, as I was not connecting with Eileen as often as I would like. The disappointment in me lowered my vibration even more, and that in turn made it even harder to connect. I had become very negative about the chances of doing the walk, as it felt there were powers in place that were intent on preventing me from doing it.

And apart from that, this book I was supposed to be writing had come to a complete standstill, and not a word had been written for several months.

I sat down one night and voiced my annoyance strongly, then asked Eileen what the hell was going on. I was surprised and delighted when I started receiving her message, which, as usual, was insightful and comforting. She said:

> This is a period of cleansing in preparation for your journey, whenever that may take place. It is important for you to clear any physical debris so that you can concentrate solely on the journey, without distractions, and to this end, all distractions, especially the physical ones, need to be cleared.
>
> When you walk across the Iberian Peninsula, you will encounter many objectives that will require your undivided attention, for this journey will be pivotal in your growth as a soul and in the enhancement of our connection.
>
> The book may seem to be on hold at the moment, but this is how it should be, for there is a veritable mountain of information that will come your way whilst traversing Spain. Do not look at this time as a setback; see it as a part of the preparation for the most important event in this lifetime. You will see that the events occurring at present are a necessary part of that journey's preparation.
>
> Be positive; there are always lessons to be learnt from every situation, but it is for you to search out and learn from those lessons.
>
> All is well, even if it does not appear that way to you, and you are on your path to so much more enlightenment than you can possibly imagine. Be patient; try to step back and view the situation from afar, and then the lessons will become clear.
>
> We are all here, watching your progress and sending encour-

agement and love—Divine love that is the power of the Universe.

It is so important for us to keep our vibration high so we can make these incredible connections, and as Eileen says, we need to try to understand the reasons behind situations that come our way. But it is equally important to recognise that we are only human and will have times when we slip back into our old ways and drop our vibration.

If we can recognise those times, we can reverse them and seek joy to raise our vibration and connect once again.

Chapter 12

Believing Is Seeing

As I have previously said, the day I met Eileen was the single most important event in my life. I had been drifting along before without any real direction, and she gave my life purpose. Eileen was the love of my life; she brought light into my life. She was my inspiration, my confidant, my partner, and so much more. When she transitioned, I was sure we would connect in some way, and that belief helped to make the connection so much easier.

When we truly believe that our loved ones are around us and wanting to connect, we will start to see the evidence of their presence, not just with the eyes, but seeing and understanding through the thoughts that come into our head. Believing makes us more aware and receptive, which enables us to see or feel the energies that are around us and see and recognise the signs our loved ones bring us, and it allows us to see the truth of the Universe that we are all spiritual beings having a human experience. This human cloak that we wear is just a temporary residence, and the life we experience now is only one of many throughout our spiritual and universal existence. It is important that we have the right balance in our lives, and we should not spend all our time focusing on the spiritual aspects, but neither should we be separated from them. This is what Eileen once said to me:

Believing Is Seeing

" We are all from the same source and therefore are all connected. Those you loved in this lifetime who have returned home are still from that same source and have that same connection with you; only now they are nonphysical and reside in spirit—the dimension of bliss. This bliss can be yours when you connect with us and you get that complete validation that we are indeed with you, right here, right now. When you realise this and have one of those "light bulb" moments, the most ecstatic feeling of joy will fill you. Be on the lookout for us always, but don't detract from your Earth processes; just be aware, and we will be there.

Life on Earth should be a balance of both physical and spiritual aspects of your being, because the soul needs both aspects to grow. If too much emphasis is placed on the physical, then a separation can occur and you can feel apart from Source. If there is too much focus on spirit, then the whole purpose of incarnating is lost. The perfect blending of physical and spiritual aspects enhances your life and soul.

I want to stress again that connecting with those in spirit is not just for the chosen few, the so-called gurus or psychics; it is available for everyone. We can all connect if we believe unequivocally they are here with us. Just as we all know that the sun will rise tomorrow to bring us a new day, that absolute believing will allow us to see the signs, thoughts, and feelings that confirm their presence, along with the comfort it brings in the realisation that we are truly immortal beings who traverse the dimensions and continue to grow, that death as we know it is not the final destination but purely a time of transition from physical to spirit, just as birth is a transition from spirit to physical.

There will, no doubt, be those who will say that all this is just wishful thinking and that it is not real, but what is reality?

We perceive the world around us to be reality because we can see it, feel it and touch it. But is this life we live on Earth a reality, or is it just an act of play as part of our total existence—the existence we have been living with this cycle of physical and spiritual lives for centuries? Many spiritual books tell us that we can create our own reality and that we can manifest events and bring things into our lives. If this is true, is this life a reality, or is it all just an illusion conjured up by the power of our minds, both consciously and unconsciously?

I certainly don't have the answer to that, but what I do know is that the events that occurred after Eileen's transition were not something that I consciously planned. They were not something I even visualised, but they have been so important to me and have been instrumental in overcoming my grief and moving forward in my life. Regardless of whether I have unconsciously manifested all that has happened to me since Eileen's transition or not, I totally believe she is with me now and always, and because I believe I see the evidence.

I have now overcome my grief and have no fear of death, as I know it is just a transition that will take me across the dimensions to where she now resides, and we will be completely together again. But until that time comes, as Eileen and I continue on this journey, I hope to discover more about who we really are, what our lives are all about, and what we can do to make the world a better place. Eileen has said that love is one of the most powerful energies there is, so maybe Hal David had the right idea when he wrote the words to the song "What The World Needs Now."

If the world was full of love and light, there would be no room for hate and darkness. If we could appreciate the diverse nature of the human race with its multiplicity of cultures and accept them rather than be fearful of them, if we could come together and live in harmony with one another and work towards building a better and cleaner world, then perhaps conflict and war would be a thing of the past. That's a nice thought, but if we really believe we are all from the one source, as Eileen says, then why couldn't we see it become a reality?

Chapter 13

The Camino

Finally the time arrived when I was able to walk the Camino de Santiago. With all the delays and health issues behind me, I boarded a plane in Sydney on the 9th of August 2024 bound for Paris. My daughter was unable to take sufficient time off work, but came with me and was spending a week in Paris before returning home. At last this was actually happening after four years of delays. In preparation for this epic trek, I had been walking up to 10 kilometres most days with my loaded backpack, which weighed just over 7 kilograms, over the 3 months prior, and was getting used to the weight and distance.

I landed in Paris and the next day caught a train to Bayonne, then another to St. Jean Pied de Port, where the Camino Francés, also known as "The Way of St. James", was to begin in a valley in the Pyrenees close to the Spanish border. I had decided to walk past Santiago de Compostela and on to the west coast of Spain at Muxia, then Fisterra, known in times past as the end of the world. So in total, I was planning to walk a bit over 900 kilometres over a period of 50 days, including 5 rest days, which averaged out at around 20 kilometres per walking day.

To get there I had flown at over 900 km/h and caught trains travelling at up to 320 km/h, then I started walking at a maximum of 5 km/h. The plane and trains were all about getting to the destination, but the walking was all about the journey; the goal was not the destination, the goal was to enjoy and absorb myself in every step of the way. There had to be a start and a finish, but it was what was in between that really mattered.

Before I left I asked Eileen if she had a message for me to take on the journey, which she did:

> Savour each moment as it comes, the arduous and the joyful, for this is the tapestry of the Camino. There are many energies at work when you walk this sacred path, and the experiences you will share will be unique to you. Take each step as it comes and be beholden to the nature that you will be immersed in.
>
> This journey can be life-changing if you will let it. To enter the journey with a spirit of awe and wonder is to fully involve yourself in those powerful energies. Allow the journey to unfold and cherish each moment; hold onto the trilogy of belief, trust and knowing that you can complete this pilgrimage in your own way. Do not be swayed by others' opinions of what the Camino should be; stay true to yourself.
>
> We will all be with you every step of the way, sending you love and encouragement. This is your moment to enjoy, see positives in all, and allow your soul to grow.
>
> Blessings.

It was very hot when I arrived in St. Jean—a beautiful day, but way too hot for walking; it was still 40°C at 5pm, so I was glad I didn't have to walk that day. The first thing I did was to buy some trekking poles because I couldn't bring any with me as cabin luggage on the plane. I quickly found a shop, and the salesman was very helpful, showing me how to set them to the correct length. I told him I was stopping at the albergue at Borda. He said that it was a good choice and I should enjoy my stay there. After that, I went to the pilgrim office, where I got my pilgrim's credential, which I would get stamped wherever I stopped as a record of where I had been. They were very helpful there and gave advice on the first part of the Camino over the Pyrenees. The credential also allowed me to get pilgrim meals, which were a bit cheaper, and discounts into some of the attractions along the way.

The first day was something of a baptism of fire, as it entailed a rise in altitude of 600 metres in just 9 kilometres. It was a hard climb, but each time I stopped to catch my breath, I was rewarded with the most magnificent of views, and that was all the encouragement I needed to keep on going. Thankfully, the weather was mild and cloudy, so it was comfortable to walk in. Source has created this beautiful planet we live on, and to be wrapped in its beauty was such a privilege.

I arrived at the Borda Albergue around 1pm after stopping at Orrisson for lunch, getting my first taste of tortilla, which was very nice. There was a Belgian lady at Borda in her 70s who had walked the Camino many times from different starting points and a Korean couple, also in their 70s. We sat and chatted until 2:30, when the place opened, by which time our numbers had swollen to 14.

The Albergue was a converted farmhouse where a communal dinner was laid on for the 14 of us who were from Australia, Spain, Italy, Germany, Belgium, South Korea, France, Argentina and America. We each in turn introduced ourselves by saying where we were from and why we were doing the pilgrimage, and there were as many reasons as there were people. Some were in between jobs, others were trying to find a new direction in their lives, others just knew they needed to do it but didn't really know why, and then others had walked the Camino before and were walking it again as the opportunity arose. I knew I wanted to make a stronger connection with Eileen, with Source and with this planet of ours, but it was difficult to put into words without sounding too weird, so I said I was walking because my wife had passed and I was wanting to find more spirituality and purpose in my life.

The following morning I set off for another 600-metre change in altitude, but this time over a distance of 14 kilometres, so it was much less steep than before, and found myself walking with six of the others: Sophia and Nicole from Italy, Amelia from Germany, Kathy from the USA, Peter from Argentina, and José from Spain.

This day was truly magical, as we went higher we would walk into the mist of the clouds, which would lift, or the path would rise above them, to reveal stunning views of the mountains with the clouds below, as by this time we were heading towards an altitude of 1400 metres. Beauty was around us everywhere, and I was beginning to feel part of it, a real connection with nature. After crossing the French/Spanish border, which was actually just a cattle grid, we reached the highest point on this section, then descended through forest glades and out along open tracks and gravel roads, which took us down the mountain to our next stop at Roncesvalles, where the monastery had been turned into a hostel for pilgrims to stay in. The others were staying there, but I couldn't bring myself to sleep in a dormitory with 200 or more people, so I stayed in a hotel nearby.

This had been the best introduction to the Camino for me; the weather had been kind to me, which made walking and climbing comfortable. The group I had met at Borda were such lovely people, were great to walk with, and were a delight to be around. It was a privilege to be able to walk with them for the first part of this amazing journey, and it couldn't have been a better start.

Interestingly, Eileen had told me that I would walk the Camino when the time was right. Had I walked it when I originally wanted to four years earlier, the Borda hostel would not have been an option, as it was only a couple of years earlier that it was converted from a farm into a hostel.

There was light intermittent rain to welcome us when we started off the next day to head down away from the Pyrenees. There were a lot of ups and downs; some of them were quite steep. On one section we went up 200 metres in 1.5 kilometres, but the worst part was coming down through a section of forest where I had to really concentrate and watch where I put my feet, as there were sharp, jagged, exposed rocks known as flysch and slippery mud to negotiate—real ankle-breaking stuff. There were streams to cross, and still the scenery coming down into the valleys was just so beautiful.

We arrived in Zubiri in the early afternoon, and José helped me find accommodation before we went to a bar for lunch, which really hit the spot. After lunch José was heading back to Barcelona because of work commitments and caught a bus.

I was feeling very proud of myself; I had crossed the Pyrenees, climbing to an altitude of 1400 metres, then descending to 500 metres, covering a distance of 47 kilometres over the three days. My hips were aching a bit, but that was all; my feet and legs were fine, and I had no blisters.

I left early the next morning to get a head start, as I was the slowest in the group, and sure enough, it wasn't long before Kathy caught up with me about an hour into the walk. We mostly walked together until we reached Pamplona, where we separated to find our different accommodations. At one point, she decided to go up to have a look at a church on a hill. I continued along the path, and a little later I heard the church bell ring; she said she rang it for me!

It had been a 21-kilometre walk, but I found that my hotel was a further 5 kilometres on at the other end of town. In the evening, the five of us met up in the old part of town with plenty of cafes, bars and restaurants. We had dinner there, and I thoroughly enjoyed myself in the company of this group of beautiful souls, who were such a joy to be around. Peter was heading off the following day to Italy, where he was working, so that was the last time I saw him.

I was staying an extra day to have a good look around the town, but Kathy and Nicole were moving on, so I didn't know if I would see them again. Nicole was finishing her walk at Burgos, as she also had to return to work.

So far, I hadn't noticed Eileen around me because I was enjoying walking with the others, being absorbed in the ever-changing scenery, and hadn't been looking for signs, but every night I would talk to her about the day's events.

After my day in Pamplona, I continued on my journey. I left early on my own and was soon ascending the 300 metres to take me to the top of Alto de Perdón, which has a metal sculpture depicting pilgrims through the ages, and rewarded me with views of the beautiful valleys below. What goes up must come down, so I descended the other side along a track, which had parts where the surface was pebble-like rocks that would slip away as I stepped on them—the trekking poles certainly were proving their worth. I was headed towards Obanos where I was staying that night, but took a detour to the unusually designed Octagonal church in Eunate, where I met up with Amelia, who was just about to leave, she was staying at Puente La Reina, which was the next town further on from Obanos.

I left Obanos around 7am the next day and shortly arrived in Puente La Reina, which means Queen's bridge. It is a mediaeval village that dates back to the 12th century and has a beautiful stone bridge with four arches spanning the river Arga, which the queen of the time apparently had built to help pilgrims cross the river. The water was very still when I was there, which made a perfect reflection and a really great picture.

A short while later I met up with Amelia and Sophia. Sophia was having trouble with blisters, which were giving her some pain. I told her about the blister wool I had brought with me to use if I got blisters. It is merino wool that contains natural lanolin and, although I had no personal experience with it, I had bought it because there were some very good reviews about it. We stopped at a bench for a break, and I gave her some to put on her blisters. I had 5 packs, so I told her to keep one. Within a few minutes she said there was no pain, and she never had a problem after that. She called it miracle wool; it seemed to be just that, as others I gave it to had the same result. We walked together to Estella, where we were all staying, and in the evening we met up for a very nice relaxing dinner.

The following day, I had been walking for a while when Sophia caught up with me and asked me if I would mind telling her more about the spiritual aspect of why I was walking the Camino. I said I didn't go into details before, as it can sound a bit weird to some people. I told her about how Eileen and I talk, the connection we have, and some of the signs I get. She said she didn't find it weird at all, was very interested, and asked quite a few questions, then told me that what I had told her had given her hope. We had interesting conversation and met up with Amelia along the way. The time went in quickly, and it wasn't long before we arrived in Los Arcos, where a street party and bull run were being prepared.

After I left Los Arcos, the path took me through several beautiful valleys and into forested country. While I was walking in an area that seemed to be far from any town, I heard guitar music echoing across the valley. It got louder, and as I rounded a bend, there was a man playing under a tree, with the biggest smile on his face; it was such a surreal experience. This beautiful music seemed far from anywhere, but actually the nearest town was only 5 kilometres away. I listened for a while, and as I left, he was playing Bohemian Rhapsody—such a magical moment.

As the day went on, it was starting to get quite hot, and I knew Eileen was with me because she always is, so I asked her for a breeze to cool me down, and she obliged. A breeze came up within a minute, just enough to keep me cool. That was really cool—in more ways than one! This was the first of many times I would ask for a breeze, and she would bring it to me.

I arrived in Logroño in the early afternoon. After checking into my hostel, I got a message from the group to meet them for dinner in the old part of town. Somehow, the four of us all ended up here on the same day, and it was great to be in their company again. We had a great time over dinner, even though it seemed the whole town was there with us, but it was a really enjoyable evening.

The next day I was only walking to Navarrete, which was just 13 kilometres away, and was going to stop there for an extra day, while the others were going further due to time constraints, so it was quite likely I wouldn't catch up to them, which was a bit sad as I had really enjoyed being with them.

Each of our group had found their own pace, and I was now behind them all, but I remembered what Eileen had said about this being my Camino and to do it my way, so I was happy to continue on my own, although I did miss their company and vibrant energy at times, but we were still able to keep in contact with each other through WhatsApp.

Navarrete is a village nestled into a hill where there is a shady park and good viewing areas, which offer extensive views of the surrounding country, with its open plains and low rolling hills. I was able to see the path I had come into town by and the one I would be taking to leave the next day.

As I was leaving for Nájera the following day, the morning was cool but clear. I left the hostel about 7:45am and started off along the highway for a bit, then veered away onto a gravel path. Shortly after, the path ended up back alongside the main road, where the noise of the traffic was not good, so I decided to take a detour to Ventosa, which led me away from the road again and probably added a couple of kilometres. It was a good decision though, because the scenery was really nice, and all I could hear was the crunch crunch of my shoes on the gravel. This had become the trademark sound of the Camino: the sound of shoes on gravel.

Being in the Rioja district, there were plenty of vineyards, and at times I was walking right through the middle of them. I had taken my time enjoying the walk and my surroundings, and as the morning progressed, the temperature was rising. Once again when it started to get hot, I would ask Eileen for a cool breeze, and sure enough, one would come up to cool me down. It was such a comfort to know she was with me.

Since the Pyrenees, the scenery had changed dramatically. The Pyrenees were so spectacular because of the mountains and valleys; it was pretty much pure nature with little human interference. It is hard to describe the feeling of being in this natural environment: a combination of awe and privilege to be there and a sense of connection with it. With the agricultural theme complementing nature here, it was different but still very beautiful in its own way. The hills were less demanding, and the path was often laid out before me, stretching out to the horizon, and the scenery was constantly changing.

Another day on, and I was in Santo Domingo de la Calzada, which is quite a large town with a cathedral and bell tower. I just had to have a look inside this cathedral, if only to see the chickens in their coop. You may be wondering why there are chickens in their own special chicken coop in a cathedral. Legend has it that in the Middle Ages, a young man with his parents was on a pilgrimage to Santiago de Compostela and stopped in Santo Domingo. The local innkeeper's daughter took a shine to him, but he didn't return the favour, so in revenge, she hid a silver cup in his bag. She then told the authorities, who arrested the young man and had him hanged for theft. The parents continued on their pilgrimage and then returned to pay their last respects, only to find him still alive. He told them that Santo Domingo had held him up, saving him from death, as the saint knew he was innocent. The parents immediately went to the mayor and told him their son was still alive. The mayor, who was just ready to have his dinner, said their son was as dead as the roasted chickens on his plate, but at that moment the chickens sprouted wings and started to sing. So the mayor had the young man released, the family went on their way, and the miracle of Santo Domingo was born. Chickens have been housed in the cathedral since 1350; they get changed every fortnight, and any eggs are given to the sick of the district.

While I was in Santo Domingo de la Calzada, I was trying to book into Agés, which was two days away. I was having no success with hostels or hotels, and it wasn't until the next day that I eventually found an Airbnb place, which was quite expensive. I knew I was supposed to be going with the flow, but I was starting to have problems even booking my accommodation two days in advance, and that was stressing me out. I know that most people would stay in the albergues and just hope there would be a bed for them when they arrived, but there was no way I could firstly stay in dormitory-style accommodation and secondly risk not having somewhere to stay.

I loved the walking, being in nature, and the ever-changing scenery. I could certainly go with the flow when I was out there, but once I arrived at my destination for the day, I had to start the process of finding the next accommodation and would get very stressed over it if I couldn't find somewhere, which was definitely not what I wanted, because I would become very frustrated and negative.

As it turned out, the place I got in Agés was a really nice cottage. The village was full of quaint buildings with lots of character, and the meal I got there was one of the best I had had.

I decided to book all my accommodation for a week in advance in weekly blocks so I didn't have to think about it on a daily basis and not be distracted by it. By doing that, I could focus on enjoying the towns I was in and open my eyes and ears to any signs or thoughts that Eileen may be sending me.

Many people walk the Camino every year, and in 2024 there have been over 490,000 who walked the various routes and had received their certificates in Santiago by the end of October; more than 32,000 of those had walked from St. Jean, where I started, and there were many others who were just doing parts of the journey due to time constraints. So even though I was walking on my own, there were often others who would chat with me along the way as they caught up to me, or I caught up to them.

Sometimes it would be a brief encounter of just a few minutes, but other times we might walk to the next town or further together before one of us would move on. Then there were times when I could walk for an hour or more and not see another pilgrim, and this was when I was truly absorbed in the nature around me.

I noticed that some others would be looking at their phones, working out how far it was to their destination for the day and how long it would take. For me that wasn't important; I already knew approximately how far I was going to walk for the day and roughly how long it would take, but the destination was not what mattered; the present moment and where I was at that time was what mattered—the here and now.

The more I walked, the more the here and now took precedence. I didn't need to know the time or how far it was to the next destination because no matter what time it was, I was always here, and the time was always now. I had no wristwatch; my mobile phone was my only clock, and it stayed in my pocket unless I was taking photographs, and I didn't need to look at the time then, as I was more interested in taking the photo.

Getting to this mindset had taken me a while, but what a difference it made to just be in the present and to absorb all the sights, smells and sounds of that particular moment. And when I did arrive at my destination, it was just another instance of being in the here and now. When walking on the gravel paths, which was often, the crunching sound of my shoes on the gravel was sometimes the only sound I could hear; it was quite hypnotic, and I would come close to a meditative state as I walked.

Eileen has said to me that in spirit, there is no linear time; there is no past, present or future. Being in the here and now is as close as I can get to that, and it's a really good place to be.

When moving at walking pace, we can take in so much more than by car, bus or train. The world moves slowly with us, and we see the detail in the landscape and can absorb it so much better. It's the same with the mind; if we can stop the thoughts racing like cars and slow the mind to walking pace, then we have a much greater chance of connecting with those in spirit around us.

I continued on my journey, left Agés early, and walked with a beautiful sunrise behind me. I was walking alongside mainly wheat fields that had been harvested, which were set in undulating hills.

The path stretched out before me to the horizon. It was a beautiful day with wispy clouds and a comfortable walking temperature. I was feeling really good and enjoying being in nature; for the most part I was on my own, with the occasional pilgrim passing me from time to time, but I knew I wasn't really on my own. I knew Eileen was with me every step of the way, and she had confirmed that when she brought me the cool breeze and other signs.

I was heading to Burgos, which is the biggest city on the Camino Francés, and after a couple of hours in the country, I reached the outskirts of the city and walked through a large industrial area before arriving in the city proper. In a way this was a good thing, as it was a slower transition from the quiet of the countryside to the noise of the city and allowed me to become a bit accustomed to it.

Once I had checked into my hostel, I had a look at the cathedral, which is massive and very ornate. It really dominates the city—an expression of the power of the church. I didn't go in, as there was a ten-euro admission fee, which I felt was a bit too much, so I went walking around the city. After all, what else would you do after walking all morning but walk some more!

There was a bit of a climb to a lookout that gave great views of the city and beyond. Back in the city I was amongst the hustle and bustle of city life, but I have never been a fan of big cities and was really looking forward to leaving and getting back into nature, as I always felt so much more comfortable there.

On leaving Burgos the next morning, I followed tree-lined paths alongside the river. It didn't take long to leave the city behind, and I was once more in the countryside. The first section was mainly close to main roads and passed under some major intersections, but once I was past them all, it was back into open country, and soon I was entering the Meseta Plateau, which is a high plain at an altitude of between 800 and 900 metres and covers a large part of Spain's interior. The section I was going to walk was about 180 kilometres between Burgos and Léon. This had been much talked about as the most boring part of the journey because of its apparently unchanging treeless scenery; some would even skip this section and catch a bus between the cities, but I was really looking forward to this, as there were few hills to tackle and I could really relax into the walking.

It would take me nine days to walk this section, and they were nine days that I will always cherish. With the terrain levelling out for the most part, I could just walk without effort and be lost in my thoughts. Despite what had been said, I found the scenery to be mesmerising—all that open space and a huge sky above, quite often a deep blue. The scenery was constantly changing; there were shrubs of many varieties and sizes, and the wheat fields were interspersed with sunflower fields and other crops, along with natural undisturbed areas, giving a patchwork of different colours, as some fields had been turned over and others still had the wheat stubble. There were many shades of greens, browns and yellows.

When I came to the top of a hill, the path would stretch out and snake its way through the fields all the way to the horizon. This was big country, and I was totally captivated by it. The wide expanses reminded me of some inland parts of Australia. I absolutely loved it, and this was where I felt closest to spirit.

I constantly talked to Eileen, would ask for signs, and generally immersed myself in the moment. I could not believe anyone would want to miss this, but they say that beauty is in the eye of the beholder, so there would be places that don't appeal to me that others would be enraptured by. For instance, I would rather be walking in nature than in the midst of a city, whereas others just love city life.

The first town I stayed in on the Meseta was Hornillos del Camino, which was about 21 kilometres from Burgos. It had just one main street lined with stone-clad buildings; many had flower baskets hanging from them, which gave a lovely splash of colour. The hostel I stayed in was very good; I was warmly welcomed by the owner, who showed me to my room, which had a phrase in Spanish on the wall. It said, "Sé el cambio que quieres ver en el mundo", which means "Be the change you want to see in the world". Such a nice sentiment.

As I continued my journey across the Meseta, I passed through and stayed in several small towns, which were always interesting to see, with their narrow streets, often lined with two- or three-storey houses that had balconies, some overflowing with flower baskets, and were mostly set right on the edge of the street. Many of them were very old and built of stone.

At Castrojeriz, there was a castle ruin atop a nearby hill, and as I was stopping there for an extra day, I went up to have a look. It was a 123-metre climb, and the castle had a commanding view of the town and the surrounding country. The vista stretched over 20 kilometres across plains and hills in all directions, with large areas of brown grassland and a smattering of shrubs and trees. This was certainly not the boring, flat, treeless plain it had been described as; it was just beautiful.

A few kilometres after leaving Castrojeriz, I had to traverse the Mostelares Mountain Pass, which included a 10% incline and a rise in altitude of 147 metres over a distance of 1½ kilometres. It was quite a workout, but what a view from the top; the Meseta once again stretched out before me in all directions, and there was the most beautiful sunrise behind me. So much for the flat, featureless plain I had heard of. I felt so grateful to be there, to be able to do this incredible journey through so many aspects of nature, and just to be in the moment. Every step I took was a new step on new ground, every hour brought new vistas and people, the world around me was changing constantly, and it was an experience like nothing else I had known. And best of all, I knew Eileen was with me, as she would let me know in various ways: the breeze to cool me, butterflies that fluttered around my head, and many others.

Another hour brought me to the bridge that crossed the Rio Pisuerga, which was flanked on either side by many species of trees, both large and small. This was a very lush and green area, which was such a stark contrast to the open plains of farmland that I had just been walking through. Once over the bridge, the landscape returned to cultivated fields and rolling hills for a few kilometres until the path met up with and ran alongside the Canal de Castilla, which was once a major transport route to ship the grains to the coast. Where there is water, there are trees and vegetation, and the canal was lined on either side by them, so for the rest of the walk to my next stop in Frómista, I had trees on one side and the canal on the other, which was a very nice space to be in.

After two more days, several more interesting villages, and a variety of different landscapes, I found myself approaching the halfway mark of the Camino Francés, which was a few kilometres before Sahagún. I arrived there by crossing a small stone bridge, which straddled what was more of a ditch than a watercourse. There was a shaded area with a small chapel and some tables and chairs to relax in. At the actual point of the halfway mark, there were two statues of Spanish kings facing each other. Pilgrims would generally stop here and have their photo taken at this milestone and would then walk between them on their way to Sahagún.

I stopped there, had a drink, and patted myself on my back for reaching this point in the journey. I had walked over 400 kilometres, had no blisters or any problems with my legs or any part of my body for that matter, and I was very proud of how my body had performed. I would often tell my feet, legs and hips what a great job they were doing. I know that might sound strange, but they always responded positively and never gave me any trouble, which was really great, considering I was walking constantly over fairly long distances each day with a 7 kg backpack on my back. My body deserved to be congratulated.

Once in Sahagún, I went to the Santuario de la Virgen Peregrina, where I was able to get a halfway certificate, which actually doesn't say anything about being halfway; it was more about wishing a safe journey to Santiago, but it was very fancy and nice to get. I checked in to the hostel which overlooked the Plaza Mayor.

As usual, after I had put my legs up to rest for a short while, I headed out to have a look around the town. Most days I would probably add an extra 5 to 10 kilometres to my day's tally just walking around the towns, but walking had become such a normal thing to do that even if I could have caught a bus or taxi, I would still have walked.

As with all the larger towns, there were always interesting sights to see; in Sahagún there were many old buildings, churches, and the ruins of a monastery, all with beautiful architecture. Like most major buildings that were built up to the 19th century, they were very ornate and distinctively individual.

Three more days would see me complete my journey across the Meseta and arrive in the city of León. On the last day, I left Mansilla de las Mulas in the early morning and was greeted with a fairly heavy mist for the first part of the day. As it started to lift around 10 o'clock, it formed a semicircular bow similar to a rainbow and gave the sky a mystical feel—something I had never seen before. Not long after, the sun burnt it off to reveal a clear blue sky, which stayed for most of the day.

I had thoroughly enjoyed this high plain; the landscape was such a pleasure to be in, and each village had a magic of its own. Some were just one-street villages with little more than a cafe or a bar to welcome the traveller, whereas others would have plenty of accommodation and myths and legends surrounding them, but every one of them welcomed me warmly and made me feel at home, despite my poor grasp of the language, which I felt somewhat embarrassed about.

León was a city bustling with activity—lots of people, lots of traffic and lots of noise, a complete contrast to the solitude and peace of the Meseta. It was a bit of a shock to the system when I was confronted by it, having walked in the countryside for over a week with very little traffic. I was wondering how I would cope with the pollution that comes with cities and all their traffic as I had noticed that when the rare car did pass me, I was sensitive to its fumes and could really notice them. But I soon settled in to the new vibration, and it wasn't long before I didn't notice it any more. I don't know if that's a good thing, as the pollution was still there and I was still breathing it in, although I did spend a lot of time in the old part of the city where there was much less traffic and more pedestrian spaces.

León has some great attractions, and I became a tourist for the next 1½ days, checking them all out. The cathedral had a huge collection of stained glass windows, depicting all kinds of religious stories and scenes, which were absolutely beautiful, especially when the sun shone through them. Another striking building was the Casa Botines, designed by the famous architect Antoni Gaudí, which is now a museum. There was even a sculpture of a lion coming out of a drain! There were parks and gardens, streets wide and narrow, and a vast array of shops. As with many Spanish cities, the old centre was surrounded by a modern urban sprawl. I had enjoyed my stay in León but was ready to move on and continue my journey.

The next two days were the least enjoyable of the journey, as the path ran alongside a major road that was really busy, really noisy and really distracting. My usual meditative-type state was drowned out by the sound of trucks and cars, all travelling at speed, not too many metres from me.

My lodgings on the first day were right beside the road in a new estate, which had no character at all, and there was nothing much to see there. The only relief came on the second day, just 2 kilometres from my next stop at Hospital de Orbigo, where the path diverted away from the main road to enter the town, and it was so good to get away from the road and traffic.

As I entered the town, I was welcomed by a 200-metre cobblestone pedestrian 14th-century mediaeval bridge that had 20 arches, only one of which had water running under it, as a dam upstream had reduced the flow of the river.

Hospital de Orbigo was a great little town with narrow streets and three-storey buildings, combined with open plazas. It had plenty of character, and there were lots of lanes and alleys to explore. There were many cafes and bars and a good variety of shops.

I had not been so happy for the last two days; it's not unusual for people to go through all kinds of emotions while on the Camino. Generally I had been in good spirits, but I was on a bit of a downer, as the last two days' walking hadn't been particularly enjoyable, and I hadn't been seeing signs from Eileen either. I knew that I needed to raise my vibration if I wanted to connect with her, so I was hoping the next day's walk would be more interesting, and as it happened, it was.

What a difference a day can make! The path had two options: the first to follow the road, which I decided I had seen enough of, and the alternative, which took me away from it and into the countryside once more—it was great! The sounds of nature were so much nicer than the traffic. A lot of the time the only sound I could hear was that of my shoes scrunching the gravel beneath them, the Camino trademark. The scenery was starting to get a bit more hilly now that I was away from the Meseta with a mixture of cornfields and natural growth. I would be walking in open country amongst the fields for a while, then the farmland would be left behind and I would be surrounded by natural bush. Not long after, I followed the path through an orchard. Constantly changing and such a good place to be in.

My journey continued past the city of Astorga, where the Gaudí Palace was, a truly remarkable and unique building with round towers, walls at different angles, and many stained glass windows. I was approaching an important milestone on this journey: the Cruz de Ferro, which is an iron cross perched on top of a 5-metre-tall wooden pole. This is traditionally where pilgrims leave a stone brought from wherever they live in a symbolic gesture of releasing past burdens.

I reached this point on a misty morning after a steady climb of 350 metres over a distance of about seven kilometres, and it was immediately apparent that this place was very special. My first view of it was through the mist as I approached it. There it was with a large mound of stones and pebbles at its base, the mist making the scene even more surreal. There were a few pilgrims around it, one leaving his stone, others saying a quiet prayer, and yet others having their photo taken at this special place. It was nice to see that everyone waited their turn so that the pilgrim who was leaving their stone had a moment to themselves.

When my turn came, I placed the stone I had brought from Australia at the foot of the cross in the hope that I would not only be leaving the stone but also all the baggage that I had carried with me throughout my life and clear the negativity and any blockages that might be preventing me from connecting with Eileen and Source. It was a very special and emotional moment. I stepped back down from the mound and stood there for a little while just looking at this monument that had been visited by thousands, if not millions, of pilgrims before me over the centuries, and taking in the energy that it exuded.

The Cruz de Ferro, at an altitude of 1,504 metres, is often mistakenly said to be the highest point of the Camino Francés, but that honour actually goes to the foot of Peña Llabaya rock and Peña La Escurpia, which is 5 kilometres further on and is 6 metres higher at 1,510 metres. From this lofty height I had my next challenge, which was to descend 900 metres (nearly 1 kilometre) to the pretty town of Molinaseca in just 15 kilometres, some at a 10% gradient. The hill country was stunning, rivalling that of the Pyrenees, but the path needed my full attention as it was not only steep but also very rough in places. It was certainly a test for my legs and knees, but the trekking poles did their job and took a lot of the strain. I crossed the Rio Meruelo on a beautiful old stone pedestrian bridge and arrived in the town with nothing more than a slight ache in the hips, which was gone by the middle of the next day.

The following few days took me past Ponferrada with its magnificent Knights Templar castle that I spent an hour or so looking around, through vineyards amongst the mountains, interspersed with crops and natural vegetation. There were hills to climb and valleys to descend into, mostly on gravel roads or tracks. The weather was kind to me with clear skies and comfortable temperatures, which made walking a pleasure, especially through such beautiful landscapes. I was totally in the here and now and thoroughly enjoying it.

Pilgrims would come and go; sometimes I would walk without seeing anyone for hours at a time; I would be alone but never really alone, and at other times there would be many walking the path. I was meeting people from all walks of life from all around the world, and everyone was there for different reasons. Some were simply enjoying the hike, for others it was a deeply religious time, and yet others were really into the wine and food scene, but for all it was proving to be a very special experience.

I had reached a section that was described by my app as the mother of all stages; there was a steep climb from just past Las Herrerias, which would be an ascent of 638 metres in just 8 kilometres. Many would opt for a horseback ride to take them to the top; others would have their backpacks transported so they wouldn't have to carry them. It seemed like a real challenge, but I thought it couldn't be any worse than the first day's climb in the Pyrenees, and I had many kilometres of hiking behind me since then. I felt my body was ready, so I decided I would walk it—backpack and all. I think that a lot of pilgrims would arrive at the start of the climb after already walking many kilometres, but I was starting from Las Herrerias just before the climb, refreshed after a good night's sleep.

The climb was quite strenuous at times, and some of the surfaces were very rough with large rocks to navigate, but the mountain scenery didn't disappoint and rewarded me with magnificent views in all directions, sometimes with clouds kissing the ridges or blanketing the valleys. After about an hour and a half I arrived in O Cebreiro, a very interesting village that is famous for its ancient thatched-roofed roundhouses known as pallozas that date back to Celtic times. As I reached the outskirts of the village, a bagpiper started playing behind me. I hadn't noticed him, and the unexpected sound of the bagpipes starting nearly frightened the life out of me!

I stopped for breakfast there to refuel for the next section, which would take me a further 10 kilometres up to the top at Alto del Polo, which was 1335 metres above sea level, the last 300 metres being extremely steep. A bar at the top was doing a roaring trade with drinks and refreshments, which I took advantage of, and once again the views were magnificent.

My journey through the mountains continued, and two more days saw me in Sarria, which is the town where most pilgrims start from, as this was just over the 100-kilometre distance required to walk to receive the Compostela certificate. I went to the hostel to check in and was told there would be a ten-minute wait before I could go to my room. This extended out to about half an hour, so the host kept bringing me mini croissants dipped in hot chocolate while I was waiting, which was really nice of him. I could have waited for hours! I had met many people on my travels, and most were very nice and friendly, probably because we had the Camino as something we were all doing in common, and that created a kind of bond.

But there are always exceptions to the rule, and I met one while I was enjoying my chocolate treats, waiting for my room to be ready. An American guy arrived and wanted to get a room; the host spoke broken English, certainly much better than my Spanish, but we had been able to communicate, and he was very helpful. When he worked out that the American hadn't booked and needed a room, he got it organised. But when he had finished talking to him, the American said, "Speak English; I'm from the United States"—I couldn't believe my ears. What sort of arrogance demands that someone speak English when in Spain! This was the second time I had come across this kind of attitude, which gives Americans a bad name, and that is sad because most Americans I met were really nice people.

One such person was a lady I met on the first day out of Sarria. I had stopped to take a photograph when she did the same. I made a comment about how nice the scene was, and we started chatting. She was very excited to be doing the walk but was almost apologising for firstly being American, as she had heard stories about some of the not-so-nice ones, and secondly because she was only starting in Sarria. She had told me she was a nurse and loved her job, as she felt she was giving help to those who needed it, and she and a friend had a couple of weeks free to do the walk. I said to her that she had no reason to feel bad about being American, because firstly she was who she was, and from what she had told me, she was a very caring person. I told her that I had met some very friendly Americans, that every nationality had its mix of good and bad, and that I was sure there would be those from Australia or any other country that were also obnoxious.

While we were walking, another pilgrim joined us, and, for a while, we had interesting conversations. But then he said that to be a real pilgrim, you had to stay in dormitories and walk the whole way, not just the last 100 kilometres, which was the minimum requirement to obtain a certificate, because that is what he had done. I could see this was not making the lady feel good because she was doing none of those things, so I replied that the mark of a true pilgrim was what was in their heart. If you are excited by the journey and are kind to others, that, to me, is the mark of a true pilgrim. You can even stay in 5-star hotels if you want; you don't have to stay in dormitories and be subjected to snoring and other bodily sounds every night, or to be woken at 4am by those who want to make an early start and don't have the courtesy to keep the noise down, and you don't have to walk the full Camino path. It makes no difference, because not everyone has the luxury of taking a month or more to walk the whole Camino Francés from St. Jean to Santiago, or any of the other Caminos that crisscross the country.

I said to the lady that as far as just starting in Sarria, this would still be a walk of over 100 kilometres, and time limits dictate just how far we can walk. This was her Camino, which she needed to do in her own way, and, as Eileen had said to me, she should not be swayed by others' opinions of what the Camino should be.

She asked me where I had started from and how far I had walked and was surprised when I told her I had walked from St. Jean and was approaching 700 kilometres. From that moment on, if we met others, she would introduce me as "This is Mike; he's walked 700 kilometres!" I thought that was so funny; she was such a lovely person.

She said her friend had gone on ahead, and we later met up with her at a cafe on the way. Her friend had a son who had passed away earlier in the year, so the topic of our conversation came round to how death was a transition from physical to spirit and that our loved ones who had passed over were always around us. I told them about what had happened since Eileen had made the transition, how we talked and wrote, and some of the signs I got from her. I added the comment that we are not just humans living this one life, but spiritual beings having a human existence. She asked me to repeat that while she wrote it down; she was really interested in what I was telling her.

She then asked me what I had got out of doing the walk over all those miles, and I said I thought the biggest lesson I had learnt was being in the present moment and embracing it to the full. We talked about lots of different subjects; the time and kilometres went quickly by, and it was not long before we had arrived in Portomarín, where we went to our separate hostels. Before we parted, she said that she had really needed someone to walk with that day and thanked me for being that person—it had made such a difference to her. I said I had really enjoyed walking with her, was glad if I helped, and hoped to see her again.

I didn't end up walking with her again but met her a few times in the towns we stayed in. Sadly, she had to pull out after the fourth day as she had done something to her leg, and the hospital staff told her not to walk too much on it. She said while she was in the hospital, she remembered what I had said about being in the present moment; it had helped a lot not to worry about things out of her control, and she found the hospital staff really friendly. It was such a shame she couldn't continue, as she was really enjoying her Camino, but maybe there was a reason why she wasn't able to complete it this time. I hope she gets to do it later.

Eileen always tells me that everything happens for a reason, but it can be hard when we can't work out what that reason is. The medical problem I had that delayed my trip was definitely something that, once fixed, made my Camino so much better.

It was raining lightly when I stepped out to cover the last 16 kilometres to Santiago de Compostela. The walk was mainly on roads, and part was around the perimeter of the airport, so it wasn't very inspiring, especially with the rain. I entered the city and found my way to the old part where the cathedral was, wound my way through narrow streets, which are always fascinating to me, and eventually went under a covered way where a bagpiper was playing. This time I heard the music as I was approaching, so I didn't get surprised. As I came out of the covered way, I had arrived in the Praza do Obradoiro, the main square in front of the cathedral.

There is no doubt that the cathedral is a really impressive building with beautiful architecture that dominates the city, and it was great to have arrived there. But I didn't actually feel anything special, perhaps because my journey had not ended, as I was going on to the coast, and also maybe because I had not done the Camino for religious reasons. There were people arriving and hugging each other and sharing their joy in reaching what was obviously a very special destination for them, but for me it was really just like any other stop on the journey; I was happy to be there, but that was it.

My first job was to go to the pilgrim's office and get my Compostela, the certificate that verifies that I had walked at least the last 100 kilometres. I had certainly done that! The whole process was very efficient, and despite the large number of pilgrims there, I was able to get my Compostela in about fifteen minutes. The certificate was very fancy and nice to have, but my credential with all the stamps I had collected from everywhere I had stayed was much more special—there were a lot of good memories in those stamps.

I spent the following day looking around the city. It has some very nice parks and lots of narrow winding streets with interesting architecture that always seemed to bring me back to the same place. I visited Pilgrim House, a place where pilgrims can go to talk with others about their experiences and compare notes. I was happy to find that I could leave my trekking poles there when I got back from Fisterra for someone else to use, as I couldn't take them on the planes. Despite having light rain for most of the time, I enjoyed my time there but was ready to move on the next day.

There had been a lot more pilgrims walking the path since Sarria, and at times it had become quite crowded, but the 90+ kilometres from Santiago to Muxia (pronounced Moo-shia) was quite the opposite. Over the three days I hardly saw anyone, and those I did were mainly walking in the opposite direction. I was back in the tranquillity of nature with little or no distractions. It was mostly cloudy, and at times there was light rain, but it usually didn't last long, and the sun would come out and dry everything up. The scenery was a variety of forests and pastures with the odd steep climb just to keep it interesting. One section had a 10% incline for a couple of kilometres, but it was always great to be amongst it all, walking through beautiful new vistas. A few kilometres before I arrived in the coastal town of Muxia, I got a glimpse of the sea—my first encounter since before I left Australia nearly two months ago. As I live near the sea and am used to seeing the coastline, this was a very special moment for me. I really don't know why, but I felt absolute exhilaration on seeing it. I think it felt a bit like coming home, which is odd, seeing I was halfway around the world!

I had arrived at the Costa da Morte, or the coast of death, the name given because of the many shipwrecks in the area. Muxia is a town on a promontory with the Atlantic Ocean on one side and the Camariñas Estuary on the other. At the tip of the landmass sits an interesting church, the Santuario da Virxe da Barca, which commemorates the legend that the Virgin Mary arrived there in a stone boat to encourage St. James in his work to convert the people there to Christianity. Inside, the theme is very much nautical, with angels suspending models of sailing ships on ropes and a ship's wheel on the wall, along with other religious sculptures and paintings. It was quite a strange combination, but I actually felt comfortable being there.

My last day on the Camino took me thirty kilometres from Muxia to Fisterra along this coast and was a walk, mostly in the rain and mist, which reduced visibility down to about 100 metres. I could only get glimpses of what the scenery was like, which was a shame because from what I did see, it would have been very pretty. This last day, there were many pilgrims walking from Fisterra to Muxia, so I saw more people than I had in the last three put together. I arrived in Fisterra around 2 o'clock, checked into my apartment, which overlooked the harbour, took my shoes and socks off, and put my feet up the wall to relax.

After a while, I went a further 3½ kilometres to the lighthouse on the edge of the peninsula and arrived at the spot where there was the last Camino marker with zero kilometres on it. I was at the western edge of Spain and could go no further.

I had done it! I had walked across a whole country. I had reached the end of the world. I had walked close to 1200 kilometres, including all the sightseeing walks around the cities, towns and villages I stayed in, and it felt so good. Although I had been walking this amazing trail for fifty days, I felt I could do it all again in a heartbeat if I had the opportunity. My Camino journey on foot had ended, but in many ways it was just the beginning. There was so much to digest, so many memories to enjoy, and the next phase of my life was just about to start.

The Camino

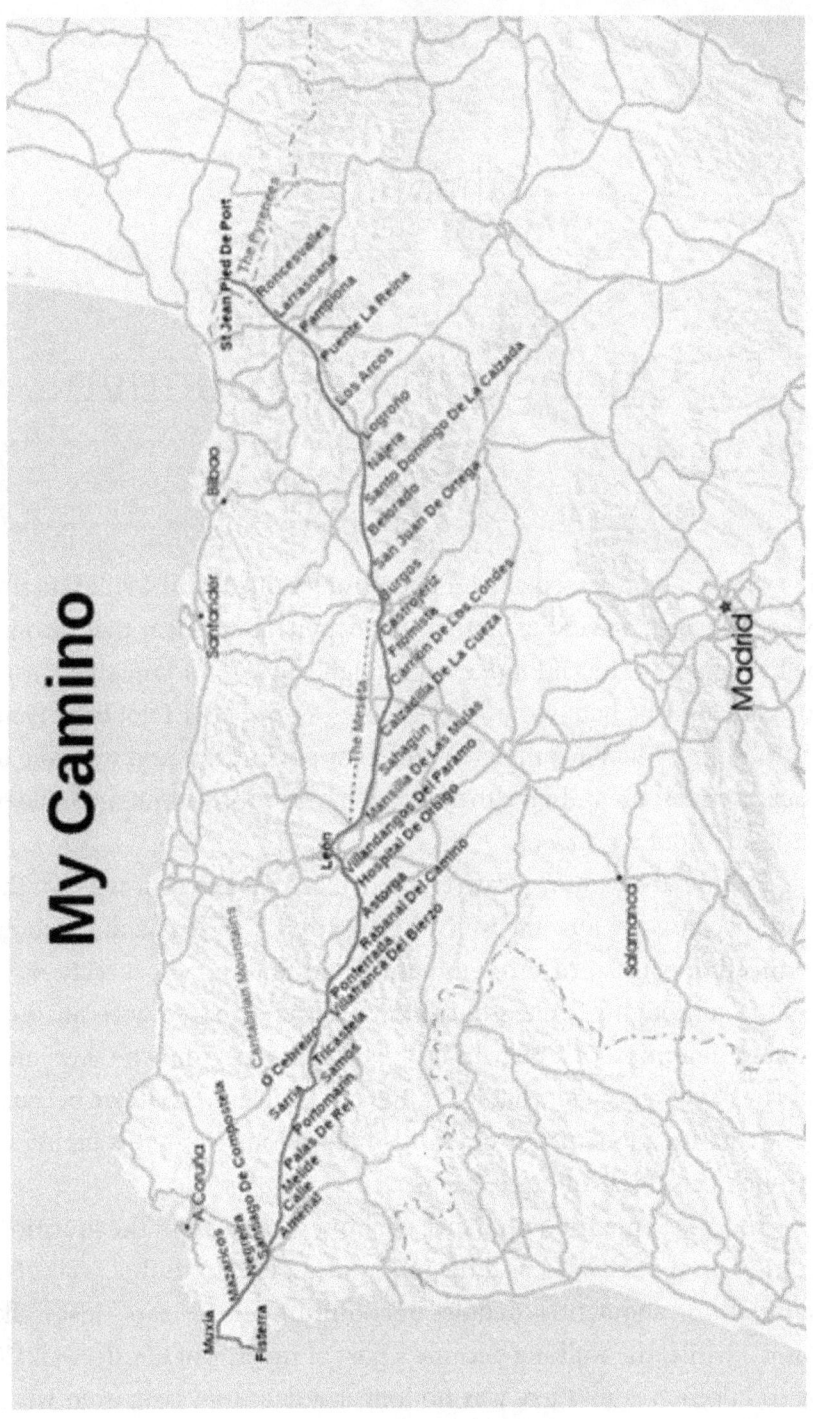

Chapter 14

A Change In Perspective

Seven years had passed since Eileen transitioned, and I still had not been able to get rid of her clothes. I had an irrational fear that I would be losing part of her if I did, even though she had told me that wasn't the case and she had no need for them now. But after I got back from the Camino, I had a completely different perspective and was able to pack them all up and give them to a charity shop within a couple of weeks without a problem.

For me, the Camino wasn't a pilgrimage in the usual sense of the word because my journey was not about religion. It was more about connecting with spirit through nature and finding new directions in my life, although I could still call myself a pilgrim, because one dictionary definition of a pilgrim is "a wayfarer, a person who goes on a journey", which is just what I was. In fact, I still am; we all are because we are all on a journey through this life—a journey that is taking us through this phase of our existence.

There is something very special about getting up in the morning, putting on a backpack, and having nothing else to do but walk. No bills to think about, no schedules or commitments to keep—just walk. After a while, the walking became a part of my way of life. To walk 20 or so kilometres in a day was no longer a daunting task, even when

A Change In Perspective

there were hills and valleys to negotiate, it was just the new norm. It was simply a joy to walk in mostly stunning landscapes with no time limits or restrictions and to be at one with nature. It is very liberating, and as time goes by, the realisation that everything I need is with me in my backpack makes me wonder just how much of the "stuff" I have around me at home is really necessary. Maybe our lives need to be much simpler than we make them. If I discarded everything that I haven't used for the last two years, I am sure it would amount to around 80% of what I have, yet for some reason I hold onto them "in case I might need them some day".

I was certainly out of my comfort zone initially, as I had not been overseas since 1971, when Eileen and I flew back from New Zealand. Things are very different now with all the extra security at the airports, plus the airports are so much bigger now than they were then. I had tried to learn some basic Spanish and thought I wasn't doing too badly until the Spaniards started talking—they talk so fast! But I managed with the help of Google Translate, and many of them spoke very good English, which was a great help. Often I would ask a question in Spanish that I had learnt from the translator, and they would answer me in English, so I guess my Spanish wasn't really that good.

But walking was never going to be a problem for me; I never doubted for one moment that I could walk the distance if I took my time and listened to my body. My body performed above my expectations; I didn't get one blister or any leg problems, and not once did I have any issues with the rest of my body over the whole 1,000+ kilometres that I walked on the Camino.

I was more concerned about where I was going to stay and navigating the airports and transport to and from them. In the end it was not a major problem; stressing about these things doesn't help and is so unnecessary, but it is hard for me not to do at times. When these concerns rose up in my mind, I would have to tell myself that those situations were a long way off, to stay in the moment and enjoy where I was at the present time. If I had stayed in the present moment, those concerns would not have entered my thoughts.

I'm not sure what my expectations were in relation to my connection with Eileen before I left on this journey. I had thought that maybe something spectacular may happen, some kind of mind-blowing experience, as she had told me that we would connect in different ways than before. But of course, it wasn't like that. During the walk, I never sat down to write with her because I really didn't have the time, but I did talk to her constantly. I would tell her how lucky I was to be able to be doing this and how beautiful the scenery was; I would confide in her my innermost thoughts.

She would always respond when I asked for a breeze and sent me many signs that she was with me, most often in a subtle way. She would bring me people to direct me when I went off course and conversations that would confirm her presence. There wasn't one spectacular moment, but more a constant flow of moments that reinforced my knowing that she was with me always. When I talked about us with others, they were always interested and often eager to hear more. I am now more comfortable with my interdimensional relationship with her. It has matured to the point where I no longer need to seek signs from her or constantly have to write with her. Of course, when signs appear and when we do write, it is always a special moment. Like the time I was walking and thinking about her when I had the urge to look up to the sky, only to see a cloud in the shape of a capital E and a wispy one beside it with the outline of a heart, or the times I asked for a breeze to cool me and she would bring it.

At one point when walking the Camino, Eileen sent me a message about one of the pilgrims I had been walking with. It was an odd message, but very specific. I knew it was from Eileen because it had been so persistent. As I had only known that person for a short while, I wasn't sure how to talk about it with her, so I decided not to say anything at that time. When I got home, the message came back into my mind and wouldn't go away, which I believe was Eileen's way of telling me I needed to pass on the message, so I contacted the person

A Change In Perspective

and told her what it was. She replied that she knew what the message meant, that it was something she had pushed aside but was now ready to work through after our bringing it to her attention. It is events like this that confirm to me that Eileen is with me, and it always makes me feel so blessed to have this connection.

One thing I had been told was the Camino would be a path to enlightenment, and I had no idea what that might mean before I went—was I going to have a deeper understanding of the machinations of the spirit world, or would the enlightenment come for a different aspect of my life?

I think one of the most important lessons I learnt was to try to be fully in the present, because the past is just that—past and cannot be changed, so there is no point to dredging up past problems, and the future is purely speculative. There are many variables that can change what the future will hold, and if I am focusing on something that may never happen, what is the point in that?

Perhaps this was my enlightenment, as I have previously often worried about future events, and in most cases the event I was worrying about never occurred. Certainly I can learn from past mistakes and triumphs to make good decisions in the present because of them, but to dwell on them is not productive. Being in the present moment is very liberating, as it frees us from the turmoil of thoughts past and future. If we are totally focused on the present situation, even if it is not the most enjoyable moment, then we have a much better chance of resolving any issues, and if it is a moment of joy, we can fully embrace it and have the best experience.

The Camino also taught me that situations that seem insurmountable can be overcome by approaching the problem one step at a time. My task was to walk over 900 kilometres, which seemed impossibly long when first looked at, but covering just 20 kilometres on average a day, literally one step at a time, over the 50 days made it totally doable. And at the end of the journey, rather than feeling worn out and tired, I felt energised and ready for more, although I had lost quite a bit of weight.

Twice during my journey I had to make a new hole in my trouser belt, and once I got home I found that in all, I had gone from being 68.7 kgs to 62.2 kgs, a loss of 6.5 kgs, which was almost the weight of my backpack. This created a bit of a problem when I was going through security at the airports, as I had to take my belt off, and there was a great possibility that when I did that, my trousers would not stay up! I had brought with me some releasable cable ties to secure my backpack zips to deter pickpockets, and I ended up using some of them to put through a couple of the belt loops on my trousers to pull them together and keep the trousers in place. It probably looked a bit odd, but it worked—thankfully.

We live on a truly amazing planet. Nature is so diverse and splendid in its many forms, and it is such an honour and a privilege to be able to immerse myself in some of its infinite variety. I have always liked walking in the bush, but this was something so different. This was more than just a walk in the bush; it was a journey for the body, mind and soul. It was walking mostly in nature for nearly two months without the shackles of "normal" life; it was connecting with nature like never before, and when I am connecting with nature, I am connecting with Source. When I am connecting with Source, I am connecting with Eileen and all those in spirit around me. It was such an incredible experience. Every step was a step into new territory; every view was a vision I had never seen before.

Often when I was on my own surrounded by beautiful scenery, I would stop for a while and just listen—listen to the birds, the wind whispering to the trees, or the rushing of a mountain stream—or just feel the silence that was in that moment and completely immerse myself in it. In the Pyrenees, I sometimes heard the sound of bells, which was a sign that cows, sheep or horses were nearby. Although not a natural sound, it seemed to be the sound of the hills and something I would look forward to hearing. To stop, look and listen is to really appreciate and absorb the beauty that is nature. I believe I now have

A Change In Perspective

a stronger connection with nature and Mother Earth and feel much more in alignment with it.

There is no doubt that walking provides a far richer experience than travelling by any other means of transport, simply because the eye sees detail that is not possible at speed, and we can absorb and appreciate so much more. Especially when walking in the countryside, it just feels so good to be there. It's not so much feeling the energies but more feeling the emotions—the emotions of elation and gratitude that I was able to do this—and joy to be in such beautiful, constantly changing surroundings.

I am not the most sociable person and have always been somewhat guarded when meeting people; it can take me quite some time to warm to them. But after walking the Camino and meeting so many beautiful people who just want to live their lives in peace and look after one another, my perspective has changed, and I try to be more open to them. The group I met in Borda were so nice and such a delight and pleasure to be with; I was really surprised how quickly we formed friendships. Even though we would have only been together for a week or so, I felt a real bond with them, and we keep in touch to this day.

Along the Camino, everyone was on the lookout for each other. If one slipped on a pebbly downhill stretch, others would check to make sure they were all right and provide help if needed. Likewise, if there was a blister or other problem, pilgrims would stop and help. There was a real sense of camaraderie on the Camino. People from all over the world were walking, and we were all part of a global family with a similar mission in mind. It didn't matter what religion, creed or colour we were; we were all pilgrims. This was where the truth of the Universe displayed itself, because regardless of what country we were born in for this lifetime, we are all from the one source and belong to the same universal family. It's such a pity the so-called leaders of this world can't see that. Maybe if they all walked the Camino, they would understand, and the world would be the place it was always destined to be.

Almost everywhere I stayed I was warmly welcomed. Even if the language barrier got in the way a bit, we could always understand each other to a point, and many could speak English very well. I was very impressed with that and somewhat embarrassed that I couldn't return the compliment, as my Spanish was so poor. It did improve a bit along the journey but was a long way short of what I would have liked it to be. When I was in Molinaseca, the host brought out a jar of Vegemite at breakfast, as he knew I was from Australia (Aussies would understand that)—it was such a nice gesture. Others were only too happy to help point out places of interest, give directions to restaurants and the like, or answer any questions. Even in the cities, perfect strangers would recognise me as a pilgrim and wish me a "buen camino".

Something I was very pleased about on the Camino was the distinct lack of rubbish along the way; it was all very pristine and much better than what I had heard, which is all the more pleasing when you consider that over 230,000 pilgrims walked the Camino Francés that year. People were appreciating the environment they were in and leaving it as they found it.

From the mountains of the Pyrenees to the plains of the Meseta, from the solitude and peace of the countryside to the hustle and bustle of the cities, from the clear blue skies to the misty mornings, from the heights of exhilaration to the depths of anguish, the Camino was a smorgasbord of emotions, energies and vibrations that enveloped me as I journeyed through them. I basked in some and shuddered at others, but it was all part of the experience that was the Camino, this amazing journey that has changed my perspective on people, the world around me, my connection with Eileen, and who I am.

The Camino reflects our lives in so many ways; during the walk we carry the burden of a backpack on our backs. During life we carry burdens in different forms; whether it be sadness, guilt or regret, it weighs us down just as the backpack does. The Camino is a series of uphill and downhill climbs, long flat stretches, wide open spaces and crowded cities; we may be alone at times and in company at others.

A Change In Perspective

So many contrasts that come with a wide variety of emotions and challenges. Our life journey also brings us all those emotions and challenges. We strive to climb the ladder of success, we celebrate our achievements and frown on our failures, and we have times when we are coasting through life and others that bring us down and test us. But every moment is there for us to learn from, to be enlightened by, and to grow, if we can just see what the lessons are.

Walking the Camino was without a doubt the second most rewarding and thought-provoking experience of my life. Finding Eileen, who bestowed on me the gift of unconditional love and the knowledge of our immortality, was the first.

Chapter 15

A Final Message

I have been both surprised and gratified by the impact this information has had on people, and I asked Eileen about this.

Here's what she said:

" The messages we bring are the universal truths from Source. They are the infinite wisdom that is available without the limitations of the human faculty. These messages are not only the key to unlock the grief of those who think they have lost a loved one, but also the knowledge that if all of humanity could understand we are all from the one Source—we are all brothers and sisters.

These messages are so powerful and important; if they were to be understood by all, there would be no conflict or strife. They can be life-changing not only for the individual but also for all of mankind. These messages are always brought with unconditional love.

This is not a religion; it is universal truth. There are no conditions applied—free will is for everyone to listen or not. As always, humans have the right to choose, and every choice has its consequence. If light prevails throughout the world, it can become the paradise it was intended to be.

www.ingramcontent.com/pod-product-compliance
Lightning Source LLC
Chambersburg PA
CBHW031953080426
42735CB00007B/373